JUMBLE® Trouble

These Puzzles Are a Problem!

Henri Arnold,
Bob Lee,
Jeff Knurek, &
David L. Hoyt

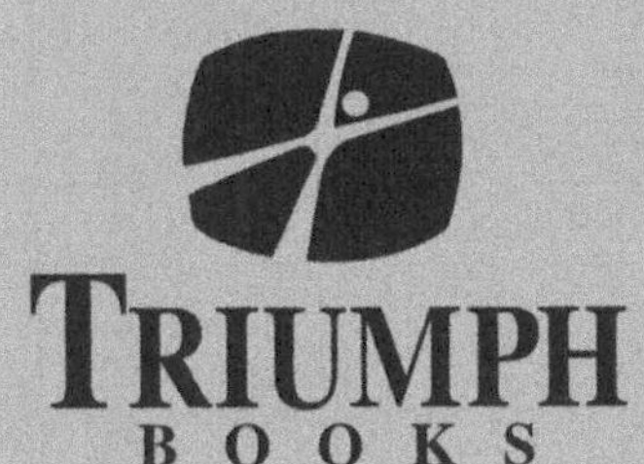

WARNING
WARNING
WARNING
WARNING
WARNING
WARNING
WARNING
WARNING
WARNING
WARNING

This book is available in quantity at special discounts
for your group or organization.

For further information, con tact:
Triumph Books LLC
814 North Franklin Street
Chicago, Illinois 60610
Phone: (312) 337-0747
www.triumphbooks.com

Printed in U.S.A.

ISBN: 978-1-62937-917-3

Design by Sue Knopf

Contents

JUMBLE®

Trouble

Classic Puzzles

WARNING WARNING WARNING WARNING WARNING WARNING WARNING

WARNING WARNING WARNING WARNING

WARNING WARNING WARNING WARNING WARNING WARNING WARNING

PUZZLE 1

JUMBLE®

Unscramble these four Jumbles, one letter to each square, to form four ordinary words.

SUMOY
HUCET
NONITE
GUBREO
WHAT YOU MIGHT GET FROM ONE HUG.

Now arrange the circled letters to form the surprise answer, as suggested by the above cartoon.

Print answer here " "

WARNING WARNING WARNING WARNING WARNING WARNING WARNING

PUZZLE 2

JUMBLE®

Unscramble these four Jumbles, one letter to each square, to form four ordinary words.

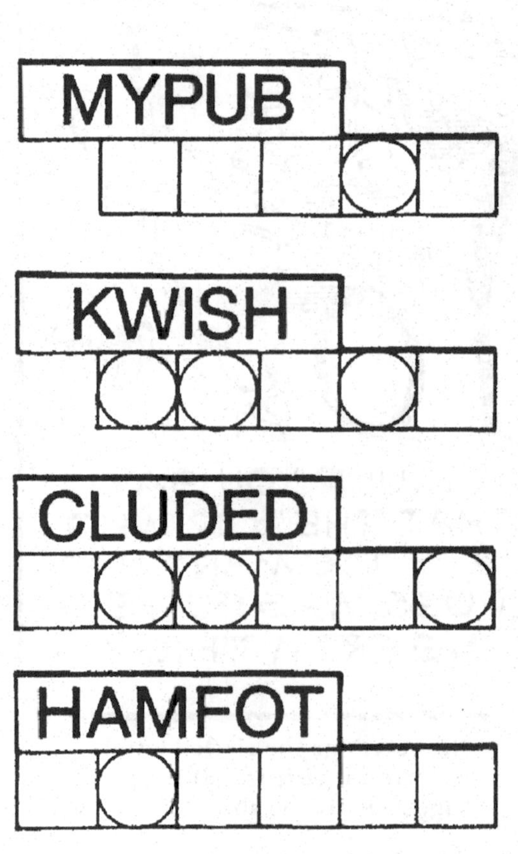

MYPUB
KWISH
CLUDED
HAMFOT

Cheer up—
you'll see
better days
THAT HOBO WAS DOWN AND OUT BUT NOT EXACTLY THIS.

Now arrange the circled letters to form the surprise answer, as suggested by the above cartoon.

Print answer here " ______ - __ "

PUZZLE 3

WARNING WARNING WARNING WARNING WARNING WARNING WARNING

JUMBLE®

Unscramble these four Jumbles, one letter to each square, to form four ordinary words.

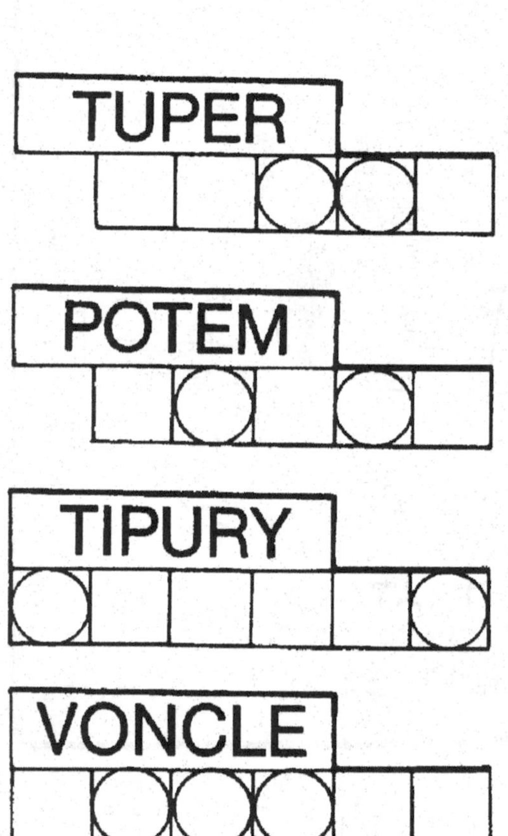

TUPER
POTEM
TIPURY
VONCLE

He's sure stuck on them
WOULD YOU SAY THAT THE KID WHO ATE TOO MANY HOT DOGS WAS SUFFERING FROM THIS?

Now arrange the circled letters to form the surprise answer, as suggested by the above cartoon.

Print answer here " "

PUZZLE 4

WARNING WARNING WARNING WARNING WARNING WARNING WARNING

JUMBLE®

Unscramble these four Jumbles, one letter to each square, to form four ordinary words.

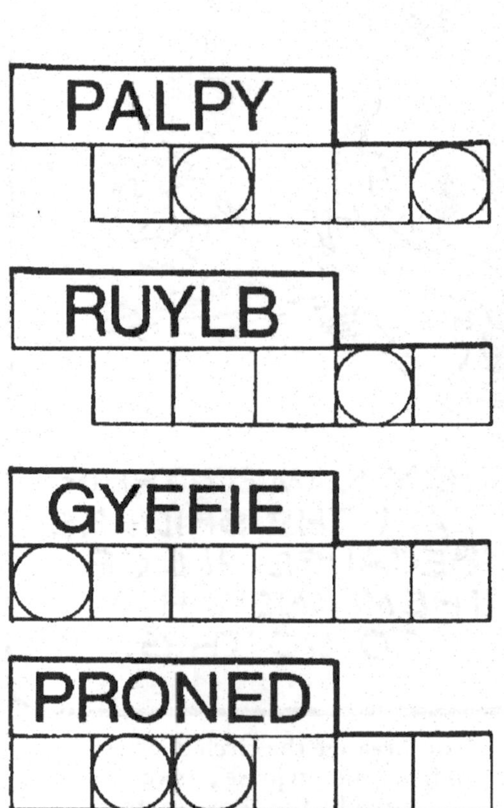

PALPY
RUYLB
GYFFIE
PRONED

HOW SOME HONEST OPINIONS ARE EXPRESSED.

Now arrange the circled letters to form the surprise answer, as suggested by the above cartoon.

Print answer here 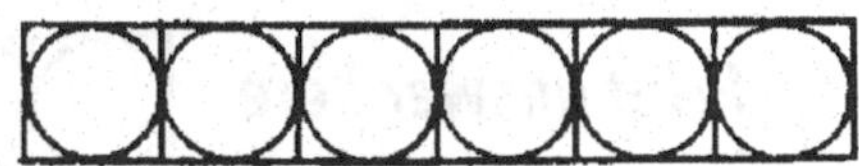

JUMBLE®

Unscramble these four Jumbles, one letter to each square, to form four ordinary words.

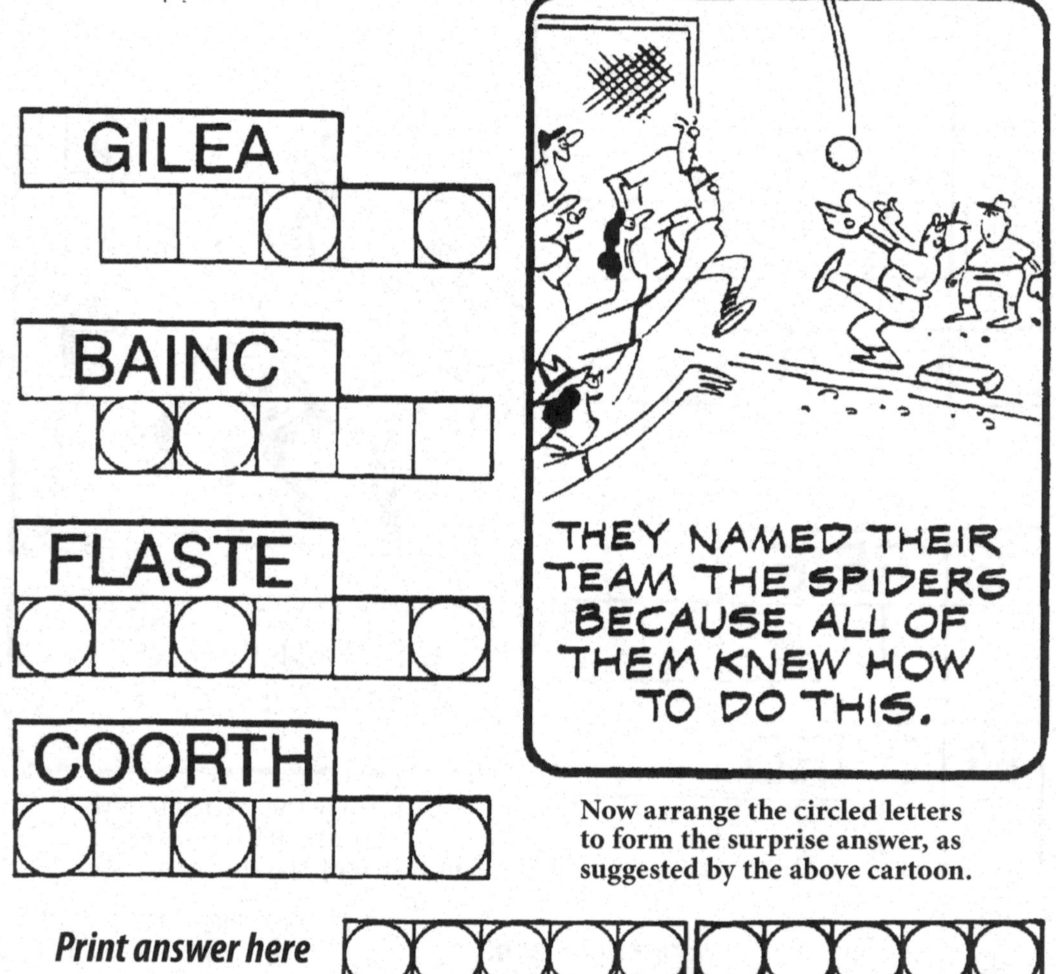
GILEA
BAINC
FLASTE
COORTH
THEY NAMED THEIR TEAM THE SPIDERS BECAUSE ALL OF THEM KNEW HOW TO DO THIS.

Now arrange the circled letters to form the surprise answer, as suggested by the above cartoon.

Print answer here

PUZZLE 6

WARNING WARNING WARNING WARNING WARNING WARNING WARNING

JUMBLE®

Unscramble these four Jumbles, one letter to each square, to form four ordinary words.

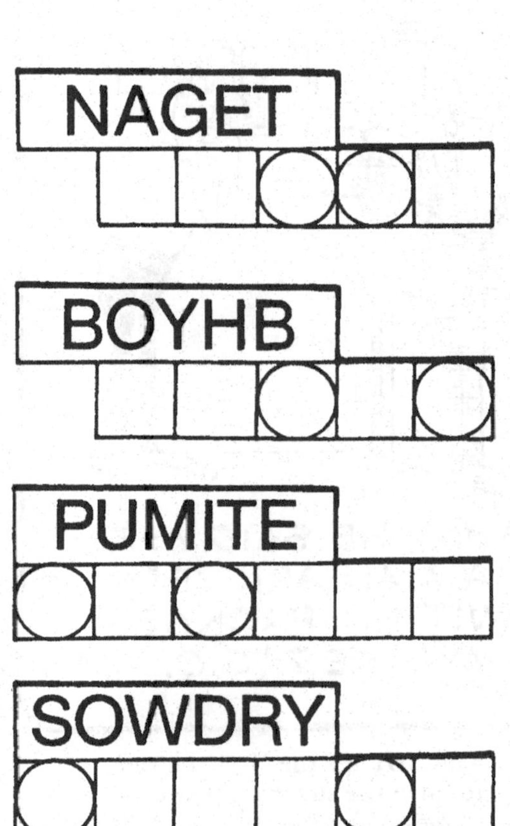

NAGET
BOYHB
PUMITE
SOWDRY

CIA
CIA
CIA
WHAT THAT UNDER-COVER AGENT WAS ALSO KNOWN AS.

Now arrange the circled letters to form the surprise answer, as suggested by the above cartoon.

Print answer here A   

PUZZLE
7

JUMBLE®

Unscramble these four Jumbles, one letter to each square, to form four ordinary words.

SYNIH
NACYF
BEMDOY
SNULES
WHAT HE SAID WHEN A MAN ARRIVED WITH A PACKAGE MARKED "C.O.D."
Now arrange the circled letters to form the surprise answer, as suggested by the above cartoon.
Print answer here

JUMBLE®

Unscramble these four Jumbles, one letter to each square, to form four ordinary words.

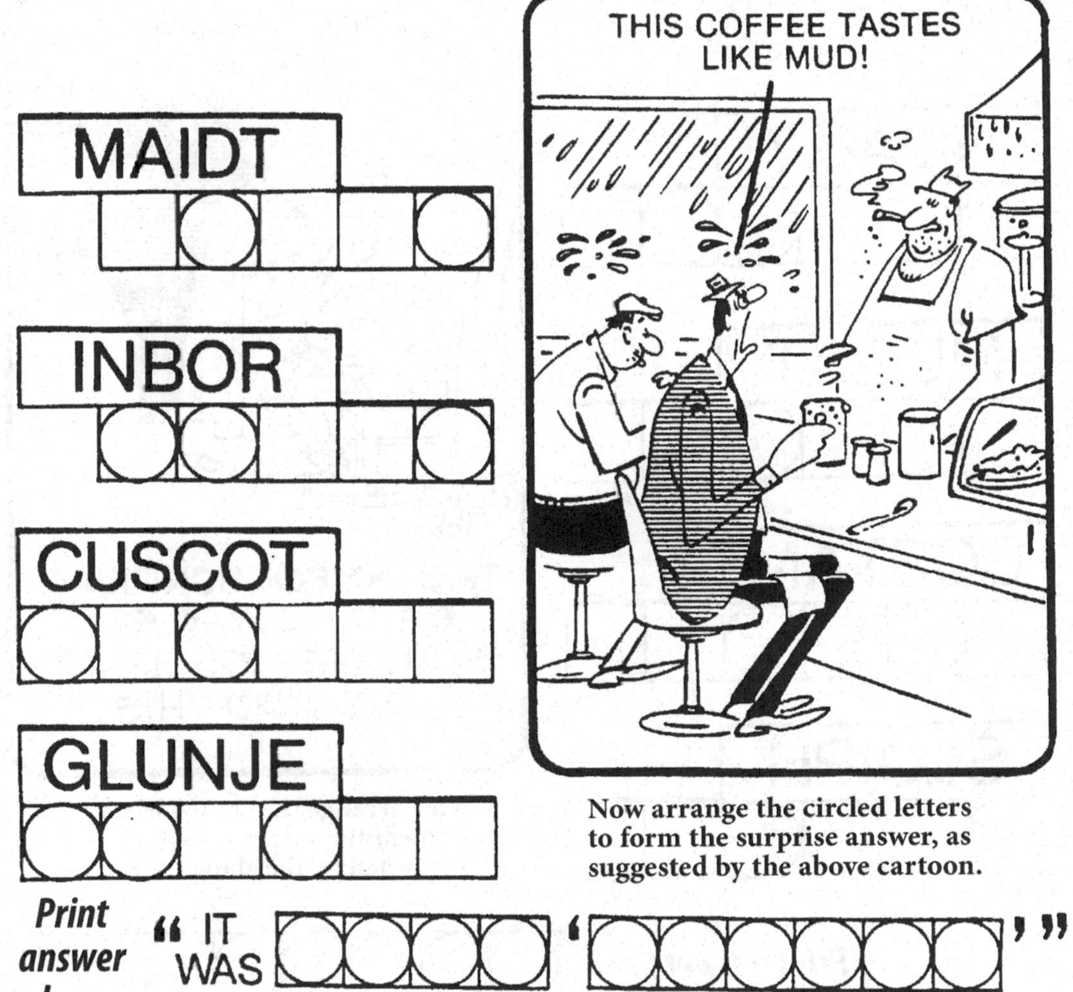
MAIDT
INBOR
CUSCOT
GLUNJE
THIS COFFEE TASTES LIKE MUD!

Now arrange the circled letters to form the surprise answer, as suggested by the above cartoon.

Print answer here "IT WAS ‘ ’"

PUZZLE
9

WARNING WARNING WARNING WARNING WARNING WARNING WARNING

JUMBLE®

Unscramble these four Jumbles, one letter to each square, to form four ordinary words.

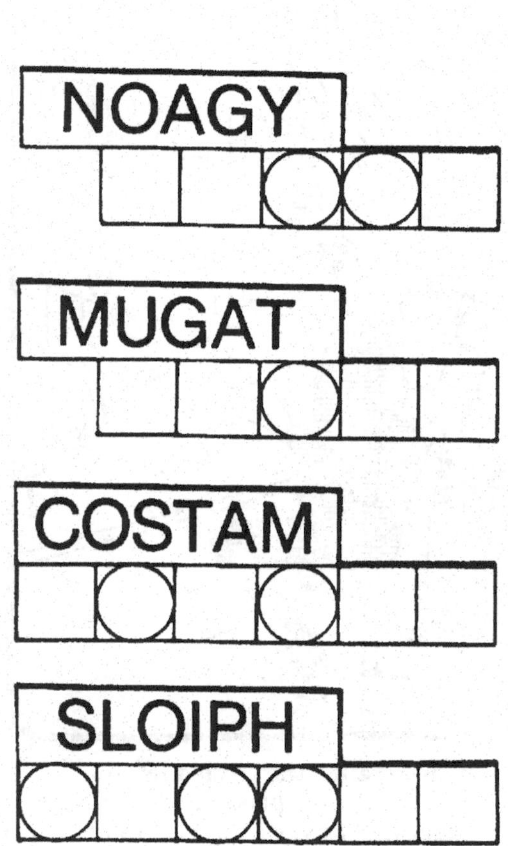
NOAGY
MUGAT
COSTAM
SLOIPH

C'mon—speak up!
THE HYPOCHONDRIAC SAID HE WAS SO SICK HE COULDN'T EVEN DO THIS.

Now arrange the circled letters to form the surprise answer, as suggested by the above cartoon.

Print answer here 

JUMBLE®

Unscramble these four Jumbles, one letter to each square, to form four ordinary words.

SONDY
ADECK
KLEETT
WHONAY
EVERY DOG HAS ITS "DAY" EXCEPT ONE WITH A SORE TAIL WHICH HAS THIS.

Now arrange the circled letters to form the surprise answer, as suggested by the above cartoon.

Print answer here ITS " "

PUZZLE 11

WARNING WARNING WARNING WARNING WARNING WARNING WARNING

JUMBLE®

Unscramble these four Jumbles, one letter to each square, to form four ordinary words.

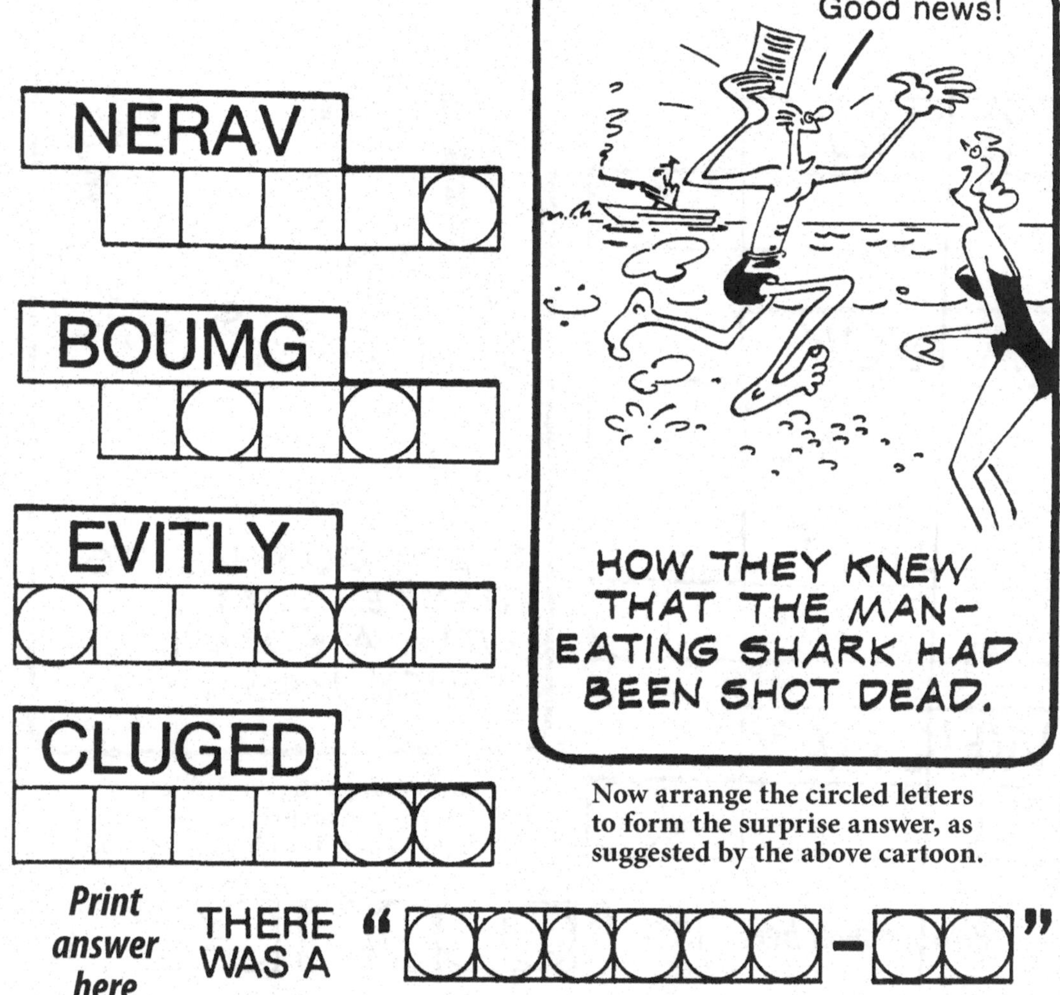

NERAV
BOUMG
EVITLY
CLUGED
Good news!
HOW THEY KNEW THAT THE MAN-EATING SHARK HAD BEEN SHOT DEAD.
Now arrange the circled letters to form the surprise answer, as suggested by the above cartoon.
Print answer here
THERE WAS A " - "

WARNING WARNING WARNING WARNING WARNING WARNING WARNING

PUZZLE 12

JUMBLE®

Unscramble these four Jumbles, one letter to each square, to form four ordinary words.

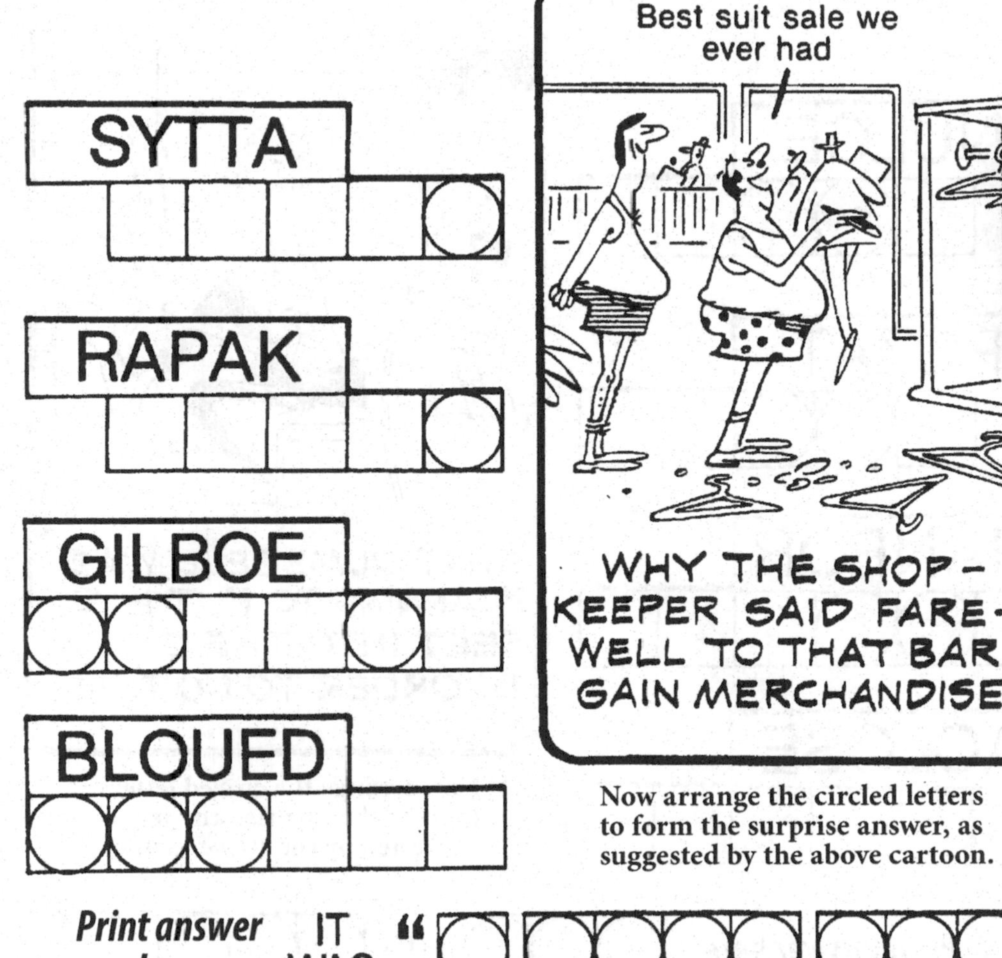

SYTTA
RAPAK
GILBOE
BLOUED
Best suit sale we ever had
WHY THE SHOP-KEEPER SAID FARE-WELL TO THAT BAR-GAIN MERCHANDISE.

Now arrange the circled letters to form the surprise answer, as suggested by the above cartoon.

Print answer here IT WAS " ◯ ◯◯◯◯ ◯◯◯ "

WARNING WARNING WARNING WARNING WARNING WARNING WARNING

JUMBLE®

Unscramble these four Jumbles, one letter to each square, to form four ordinary words.

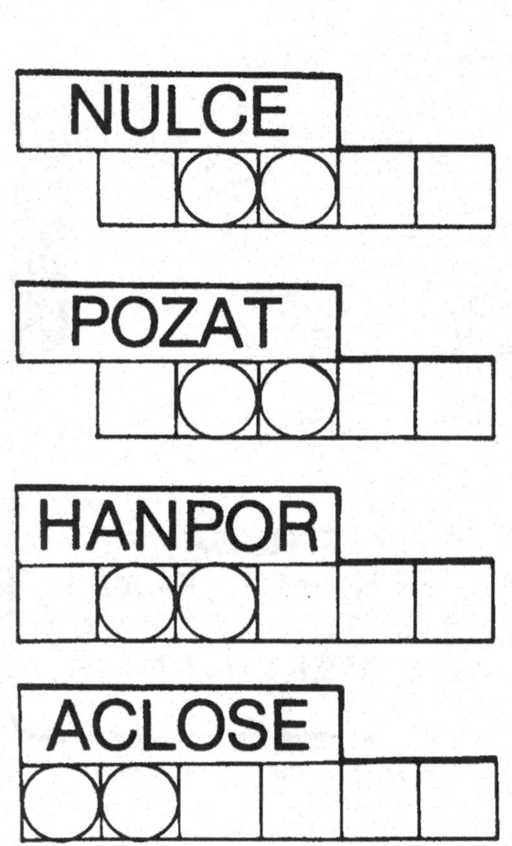
NULCE
POZAT
HANPOR
ACLOSE

THAT DUMBBELL WAS PLANNING TO PUT HIS FEET INTO THE OVEN IN ORDER TO DO THIS.

Now arrange the circled letters to form the surprise answer, as suggested by the above cartoon.

Print answer here  HIS 

PUZZLE
14

WARNING WARNING WARNING WARNING WARNING WARNING WARNING

JUMBLE®

Unscramble these four Jumbles, one letter to each square, to form four ordinary words.

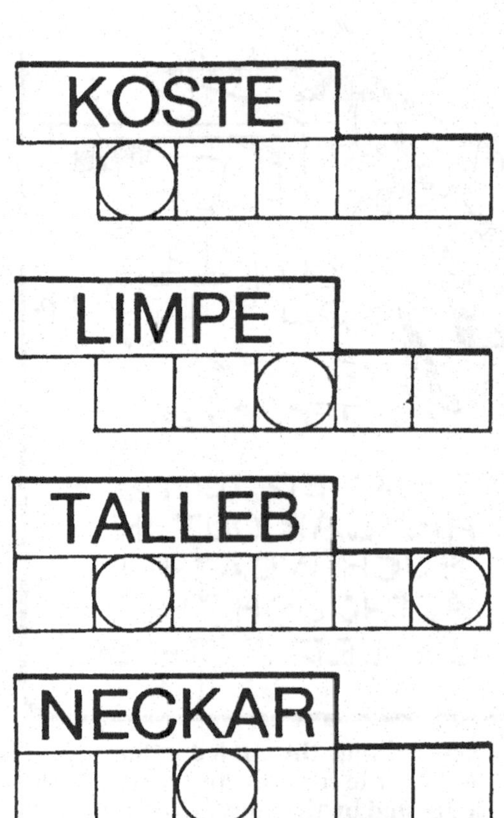

KOSTE
LIMPE
TALLEB
NECKAR

HE IS WEARING A NICE NEW SUIT BUT HIS DOG ONLY THIS.

Now arrange the circled letters to form the surprise answer, as suggested by the above cartoon.

Print answer here "  "

JUMBLE®

Unscramble these four Jumbles, one letter to each square, to form four ordinary words.

NIROY
DITAU
CEVIED
RENUNG
Gotta pick up the kid at school
HE HATED TO TAKE HIS CAR OUT IN SUCH WEATHER, ALTHOUGH THEY CALLED IT THIS.

Now arrange the circled letters to form the surprise answer, as suggested by the above cartoon.

Print answer here A " ◯◯◯◯◯◯◯ " ◯◯◯◯

PUZZLE 16

WARNING WARNING WARNING WARNING WARNING WARNING WARNING

JUMBLE®

Unscramble these four Jumbles, one letter to each square, to form four ordinary words.

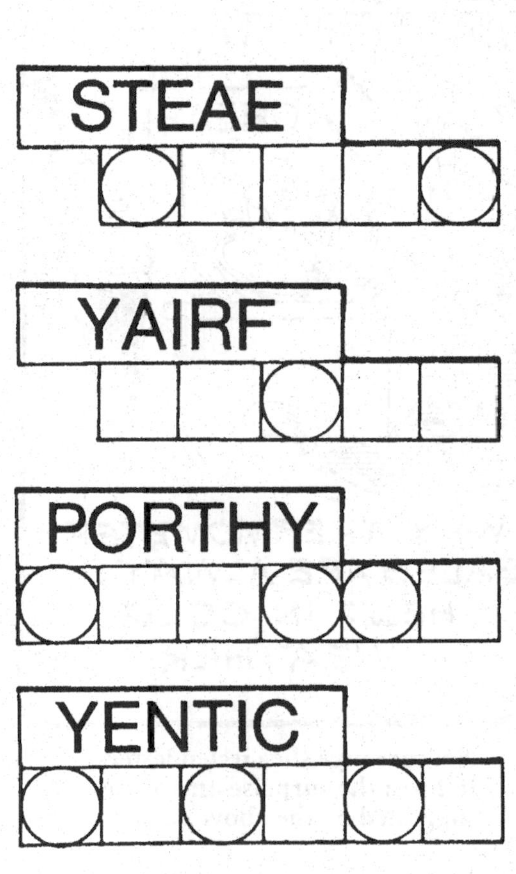

STEAE
YAIRF
PORTHY
YENTIC

What's the first thing we do when it's bedtime?
THE LITTLE BASEBALL PLAYER DECIDED TO BECOME A BOY SCOUT SO HE COULD LEARN TO DO THIS.

Now arrange the circled letters to form the surprise answer, as suggested by the above cartoon.

Print answer here " " A 

JUMBLE®

Unscramble these four Jumbles, one letter to each square, to form four ordinary words.

ORRGI
NEALK
THUGOR
RITHEH
CHEAP!
WHY THERMOMETER SALES ARE ALWAYS HELD IN COLD WEATHER.

Now arrange the circled letters to form the surprise answer, as suggested by the above cartoon.

Print answer here WHEN IT'S ◯◯◯, THEY'RE ◯◯◯◯◯◯

PUZZLE 18

WARNING WARNING WARNING WARNING WARNING WARNING WARNING

JUMBLE®

Unscramble these four Jumbles, one letter to each square, to form four ordinary words.

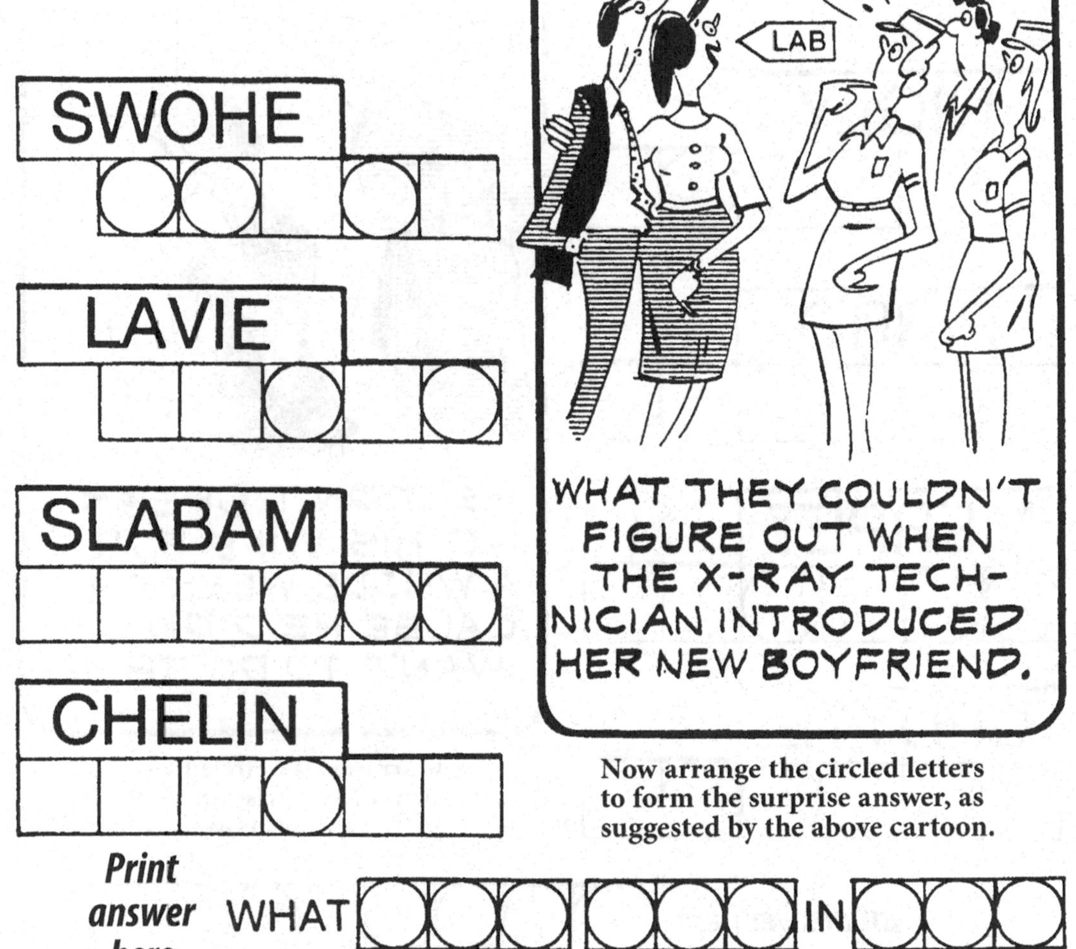

SWOHE
LAVIE
SLABAM
CHELIN
LAB
WHAT THEY COULDN'T FIGURE OUT WHEN THE X-RAY TECHNICIAN INTRODUCED HER NEW BOYFRIEND.

Now arrange the circled letters to form the surprise answer, as suggested by the above cartoon.

Print answer here WHAT ◯◯◯ ◯◯◯ IN ◯◯◯

PUZZLE 19

WARNING WARNING WARNING WARNING WARNING WARNING WARNING

JUMBLE®

Unscramble these four Jumbles, one letter to each square, to form four ordinary words.

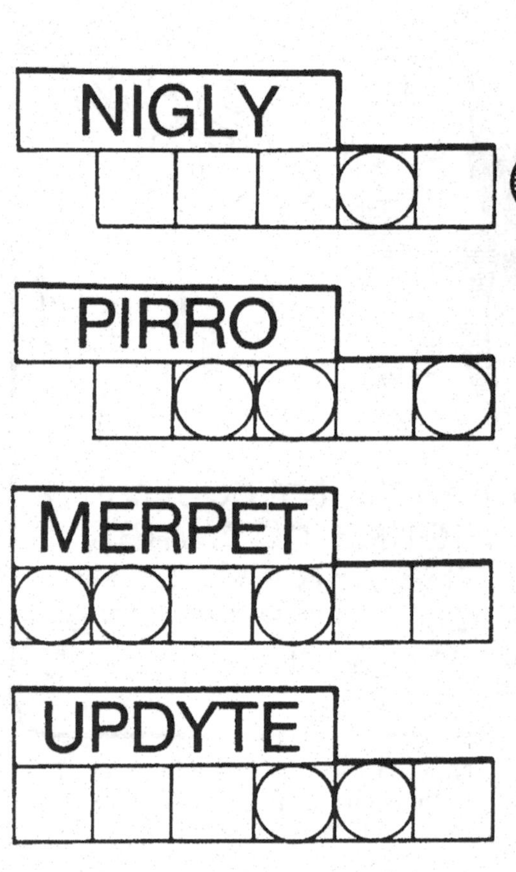
NIGLY
PIRRO
MERPET
UPDYTE

HE DIDN'T SPEAK TO HIS WIFE FOR A WHOLE WEEK BE-CAUSE HE DIDN'T WANT TO DO THIS.

Now arrange the circled letters to form the surprise answer, as suggested by the above cartoon.

Print answer here 

PUZZLE 20

WARNING WARNING WARNING WARNING WARNING WARNING WARNING

JUMBLE®

Unscramble these four Jumbles, one letter to each square, to form four ordinary words.

PLITO

NOFET

LOWLEY

GOULEY

A GUY SLAPPED HIM ON THE BACK AND THEN ASKED HIM THIS.

Now arrange the circled letters to form the surprise answer, as suggested by the above cartoon.

Print answer here HOW'RE ◯◯◯ "◯◯◯◯◯◯◯◯"?

JUMBLE®

Unscramble these four Jumbles, one letter to each square, to form four ordinary words.

RICLY
TURTE
NEMPAN
CROGED
WOULD THEY BE PLAYING THIS?

Now arrange the circled letters to form the surprise answer, as suggested by the above cartoon.

Print answer here

PUZZLE
22

WARNING WARNING WARNING WARNING WARNING WARNING WARNING

JUMBLE®

Unscramble these four Jumbles, one letter to each square, to form four ordinary words.

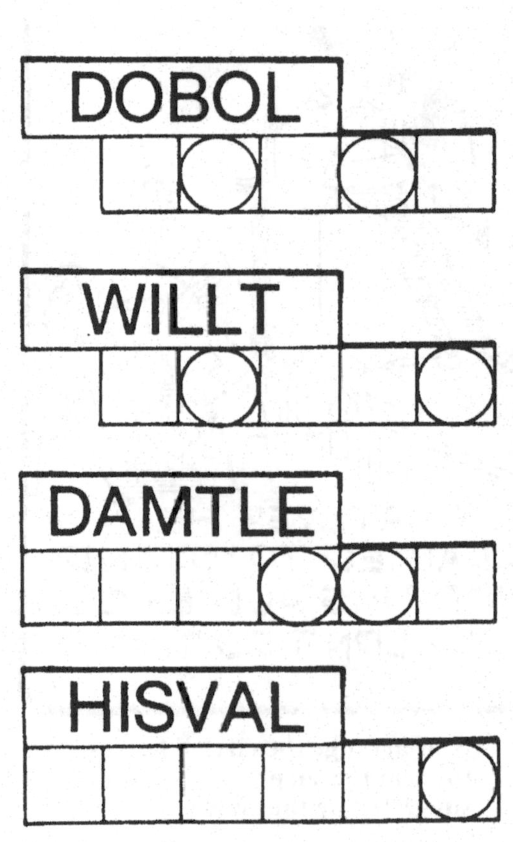

DOBOL
WILLT
DAMTLE
HISVAL

THIS SOUP TASTES LIKE DISHWATER!

Now arrange the circled letters to form the surprise answer, as suggested by the above cartoon.

Print answer here

" CAN YOU ?"

WARNING WARNING WARNING WARNING WARNING WARNING WARNING

JUMBLE®

Unscramble these four Jumbles, one letter to each square, to form four ordinary words.

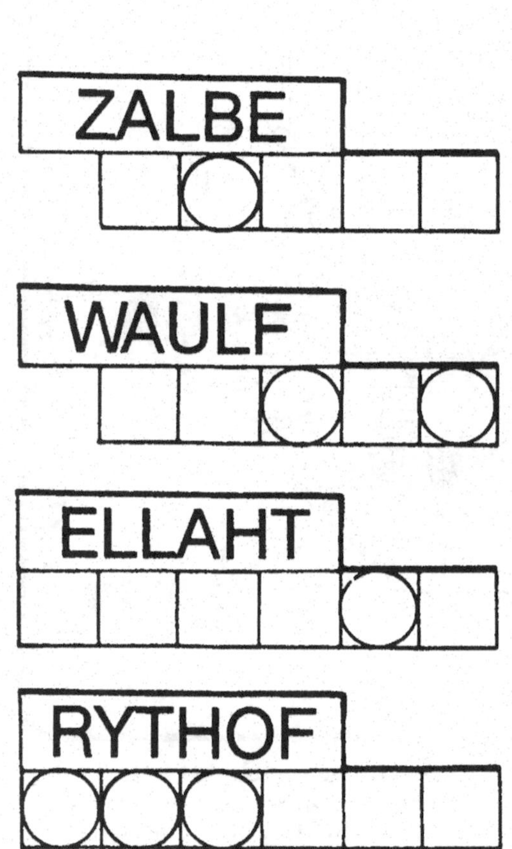
ZALBE
WAULF
ELLAHT
RYTHOF

WHATEVER HE CLAIMED TO "STAND FOR," HIS AUDIENCE WOULDN'T DO THIS.

Now arrange the circled letters to form the surprise answer, as suggested by the above cartoon.

Print answer here " ◯◯◯◯ ◯◯◯ "

PUZZLE
24

WARNING WARNING WARNING WARNING WARNING WARNING WARNIN

JUMBLE®

Unscramble these four Jumbles, one letter to each square, to form four ordinary words.

OCTIX
ENGOM
NUCCOR
OOTARR
WHAT THE COUNTESS SAID HER HUSBAND WAS.

Now arrange the circled letters to form the surprise answer, as suggested by the above cartoon.

Print answer here A "◯◯-◯◯◯◯◯◯◯"

JUMBLE®

Unscramble these four Jumbles, one letter to each square, to form four ordinary words.

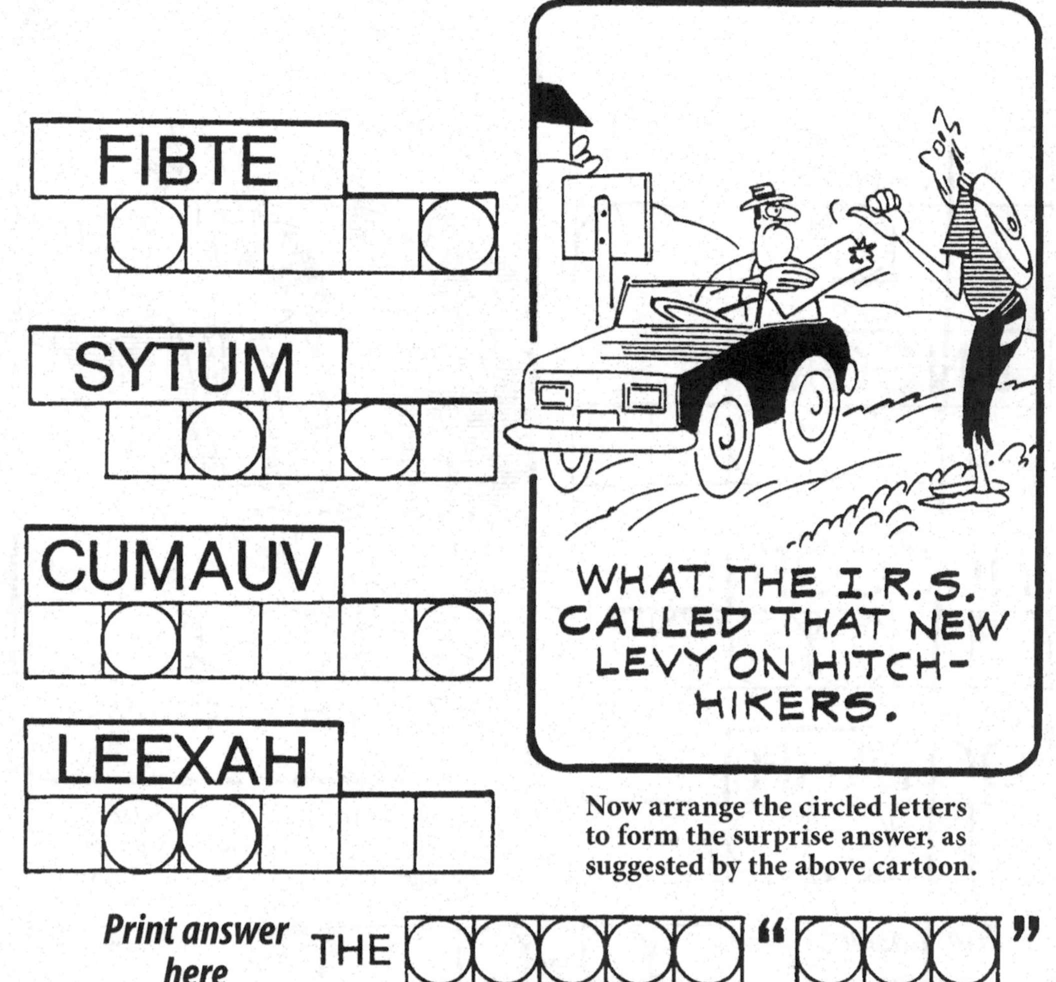
FIBTE
SYTUM
CUMAUV
LEEXAH
WHAT THE I.R.S. CALLED THAT NEW LEVY ON HITCH-HIKERS.

Now arrange the circled letters to form the surprise answer, as suggested by the above cartoon.

Print answer here THE ◯◯◯◯◯ "◯◯◯"

JUMBLE®

Trouble

Daily Puzzles

WARNING WARNING WARNING WARNING WARNING WARNING WARNING WARNING

WARNING WARNING WARNING WARNING

JUMBLE®

Unscramble these four Jumbles, one letter to each square, to form four ordinary words.

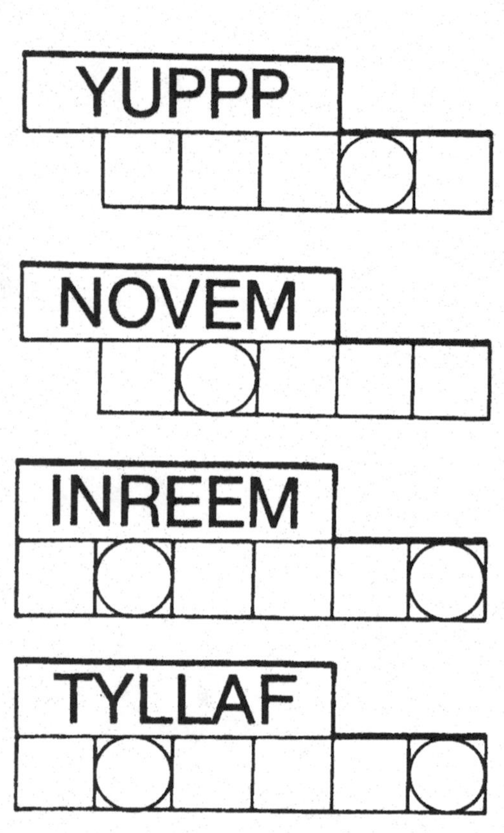
YUPPP
NOVEM
INREEM
TYLLAF

Won't be long before she'll be pitching in with the housework
BABY WAS MOTHER'S LITTLE THIS.

Now arrange the circled letters to form the surprise answer, as suggested by the above cartoon.

Print answer here " ◯◯◯◯◯◯ "

PUZZLE 27

JUMBLE®

Unscramble these four Jumbles, one letter to each square, to form four ordinary words.

DANGL
VEALE
CONIVE
HELSIR
I hear that the filthy rich don't carry money on them
WHY IS AN EMPTY PURSE ALWAYS THE SAME?

Now arrange the circled letters to form the surprise answer, as suggested by the above cartoon.

Print answer here ANY IN IT

PUZZLE
28

JUMBLE®

Unscramble these four Jumbles, one letter to each square, to form four ordinary words.

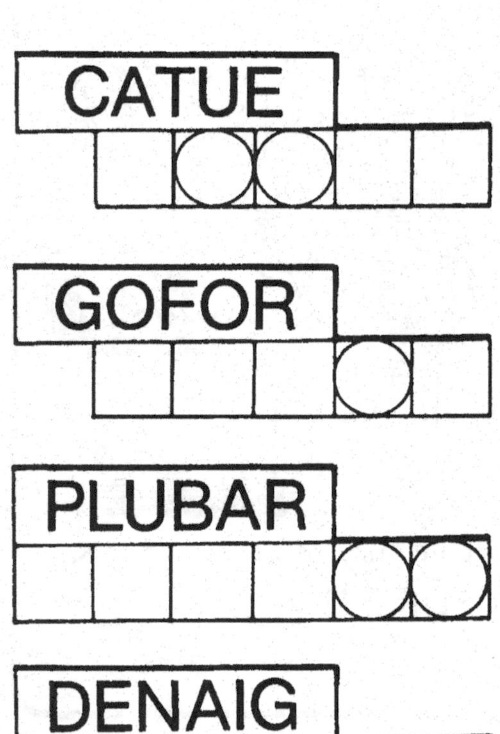
CATUE
GOFOR
PLUBAR
DENAIG

Stop or I'll shoot!

WOULD THE GUARD AT A HAT FACTORY CARRY THIS?

Now arrange the circled letters to form the surprise answer, as suggested by the above cartoon.

Print answer here

PUZZLE
29

WARNING WARNING WARNING WARNING WARNING WARNING WARNING

JUMBLE®

Unscramble these four Jumbles, one letter to each square, to form four ordinary words.

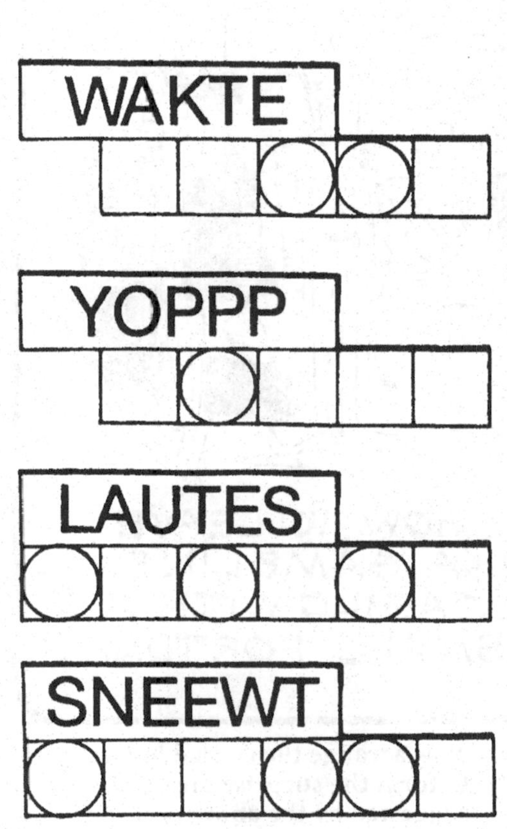

WAKTE
YOPPP
LAUTES
SNEEWT

Funny!
But ancient
2-13
THAT VETERAN COMEDIAN KNOWS A GOOD GAG WHEN HE DOES THIS.

Now arrange the circled letters to form the surprise answer, as suggested by the above cartoon.

Print answer here 

WARNING WARNING WARNING WARNING WARNING WARNING WARNING

JUMBLE®

Unscramble these four Jumbles, one letter to each square, to form four ordinary words.

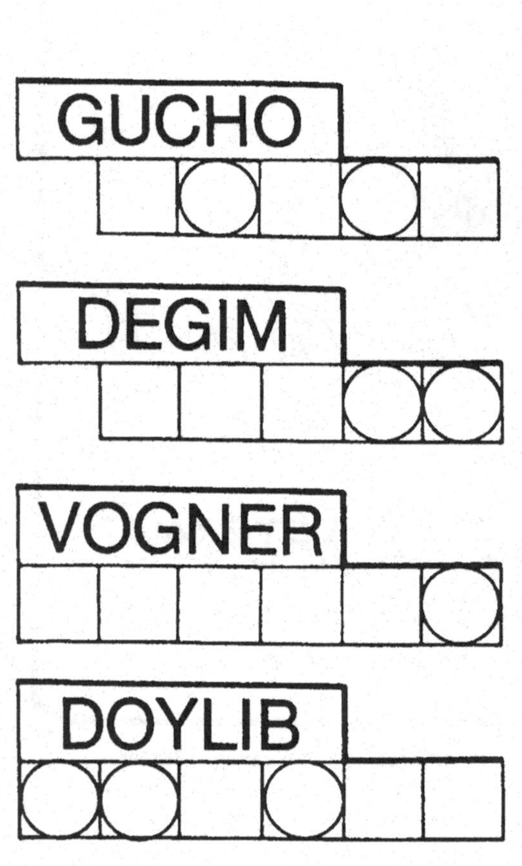
GUCHO
DEGIM
VOGNER
DOYLIB

HOW TO LEAVE
A GAMBLING
CASINO WITH A
SMALL FORTUNE.

Now arrange the circled letters to form the surprise answer, as suggested by the above cartoon.

Print answer here  WITH A 

JUMBLE®

Unscramble these four Jumbles, one letter to each square, to form four ordinary words.

RAALT
ENORD
YUNCAL
FRUTOH
An advancing edge of air ...
WHAT YOU'VE GOT WHEN YOU STAND WITH YOUR BACK TO THE FIREPLACE.

Now arrange the circled letters to form the surprise answer, as suggested by the above cartoon.

Print answer here A

WARNING WARNING WARNING WARNING WARNING WARNING WARNING

JUMBLE®

Unscramble these four Jumbles, one letter to each square, to form four ordinary words.

KANET
INJOT
PYTSHU
TORTOG
WHAT SHE SAID TO THE INVISIBLE MAN.
Now arrange the circled letters to form the surprise answer, as suggested by the above cartoon.
Print answer here
YOU'RE

PUZZLE 33

WARNING WARNING WARNING WARNING WARNING WARNING WARNING

JUMBLE®

Unscramble these four Jumbles, one letter to each square, to form four ordinary words.

DAKEB

BYASS

RETAIS

NORIPS

Used to be a famous opera singer
A very deep voice
ANOTHER NAME FOR THE "POOR FISH" WHO LANDED IN JAIL.

Now arrange the circled letters to form the surprise answer, as suggested by the above cartoon.

Print answer here A ________ "_____"

WARNING WARNING WARNING WARNING WARNING WARNING WARNING

JUMBLE®

Unscramble these four Jumbles, one letter to each square, to form four ordinary words.

TULIQ

NESOO

DELTUC

BRUPES

WILL YOU LOVE ME WHEN
I'M OLD AND UGLY?

Now arrange the circled letters to form the surprise answer, as suggested by the above cartoon.

Print answer here "OF ☐☐☐☐☐☐, ☐ ☐☐"

WARNING WARNING WARNING WARNING WARNING WARNING WARNIN

Unscramble these four Jumbles, one letter to each square, to form four ordinary words.

WYDON

DUNOB

GOAUNT

ARRETH

WHAT THE EXECUTIONER DID DURING A SLACK PERIOD.

Now arrange the circled letters to form the surprise answer, as suggested by the above cartoon.

Print answer here JUST "◯◯◯◯" ◯◯◯◯◯◯

JUMBLE®

Unscramble these four Jumbles, one letter to each square, to form four ordinary words.

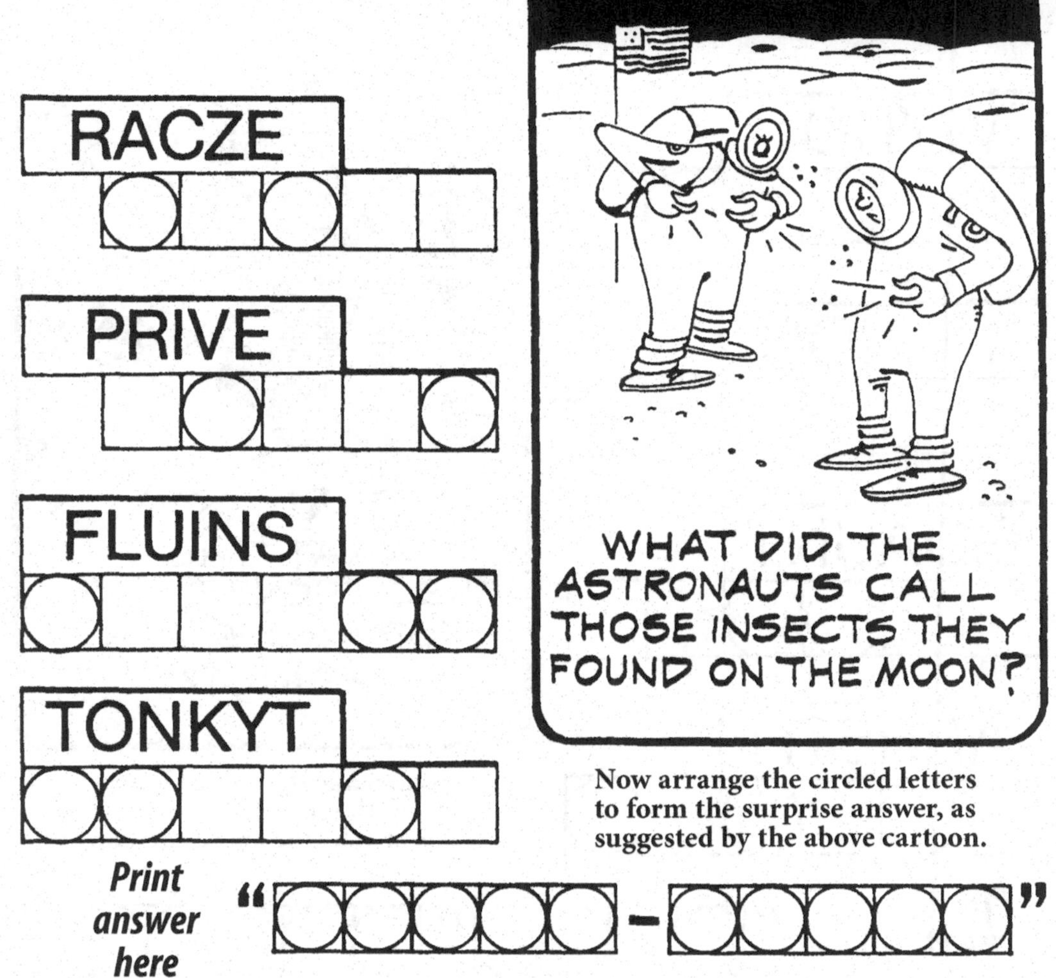
RACZE
PRIVE
FLUINS
TONKYT
WHAT DID THE ASTRONAUTS CALL THOSE INSECTS THEY FOUND ON THE MOON?

Now arrange the circled letters to form the surprise answer, as suggested by the above cartoon.

Print answer here “ - ”

PUZZLE 37

WARNING WARNING WARNING WARNING WARNING WARNING WARNING

JUMBLE®

Unscramble these four Jumbles, one letter to each square, to form four ordinary words.

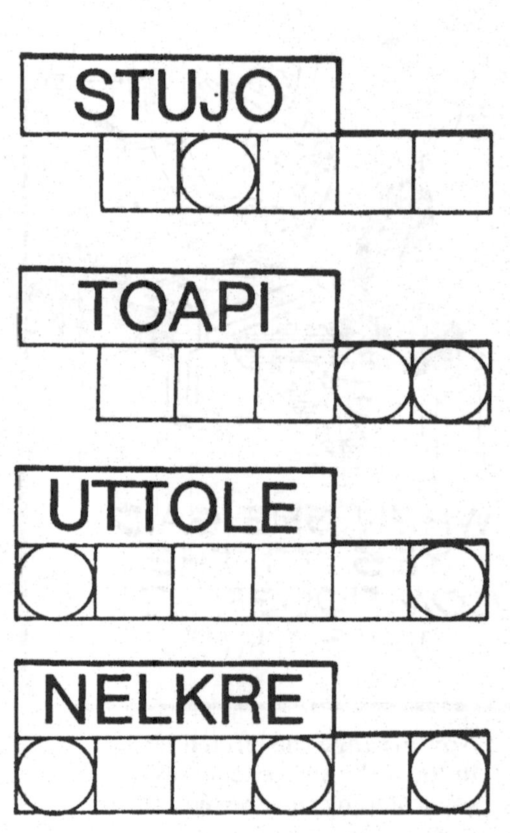

STUJO
TOAPI
UTTOLE
NELKRE

NUDIST COLONY
WHAT THE COPS SAID THEY WOULD DO WHEN A HOLE WAS FOUND IN THE OUTSIDE WALL.

Now arrange the circled letters to form the surprise answer, as suggested by the above cartoon.

Print answer here

IT

WARNING WARNING WARNING WARNING WARNING WARNING WARNING

JUMBLE®

Unscramble these four Jumbles, one letter to each square, to form four ordinary words.

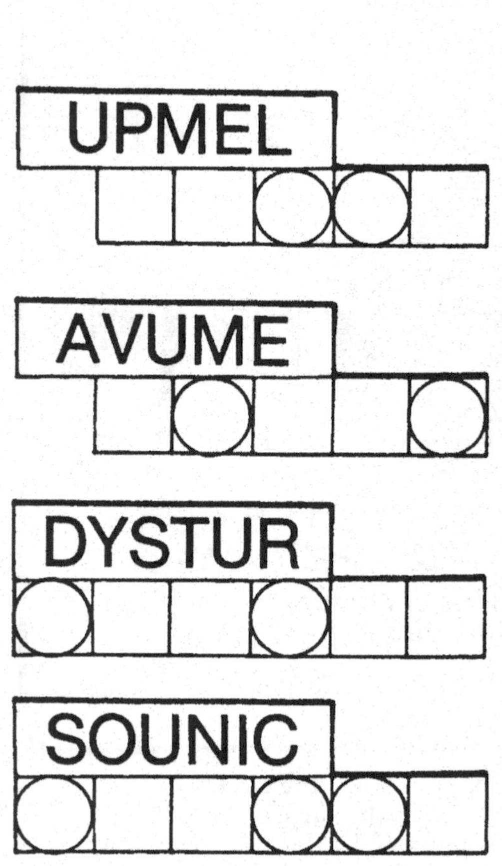
UPMEL
AVUME
DYSTUR
SOUNIC

WHEN SHE SAID YES TO THE COMPOSER IT WAS THIS.

Now arrange the circled letters to form the surprise answer, as suggested by the above cartoon.

Print answer here

TO HIS

WARNING WARNING WARNING WARNING WARNING WARNING WARNIN

JUMBLE®

Unscramble these four Jumbles, one letter to each square, to form four ordinary words.

NOUGY
SIGEE
LOYDOG
GLOONB
WHAT DO YOU CALL A WET PUP?

Now arrange the circled letters to form the surprise answer, as suggested by the above cartoon.

Print answer here A

PUZZLE 40

WARNING WARNING WARNING WARNING WARNING WARNING WARNING

JUMBLE®

Unscramble these four Jumbles, one letter to each square, to form four ordinary words.

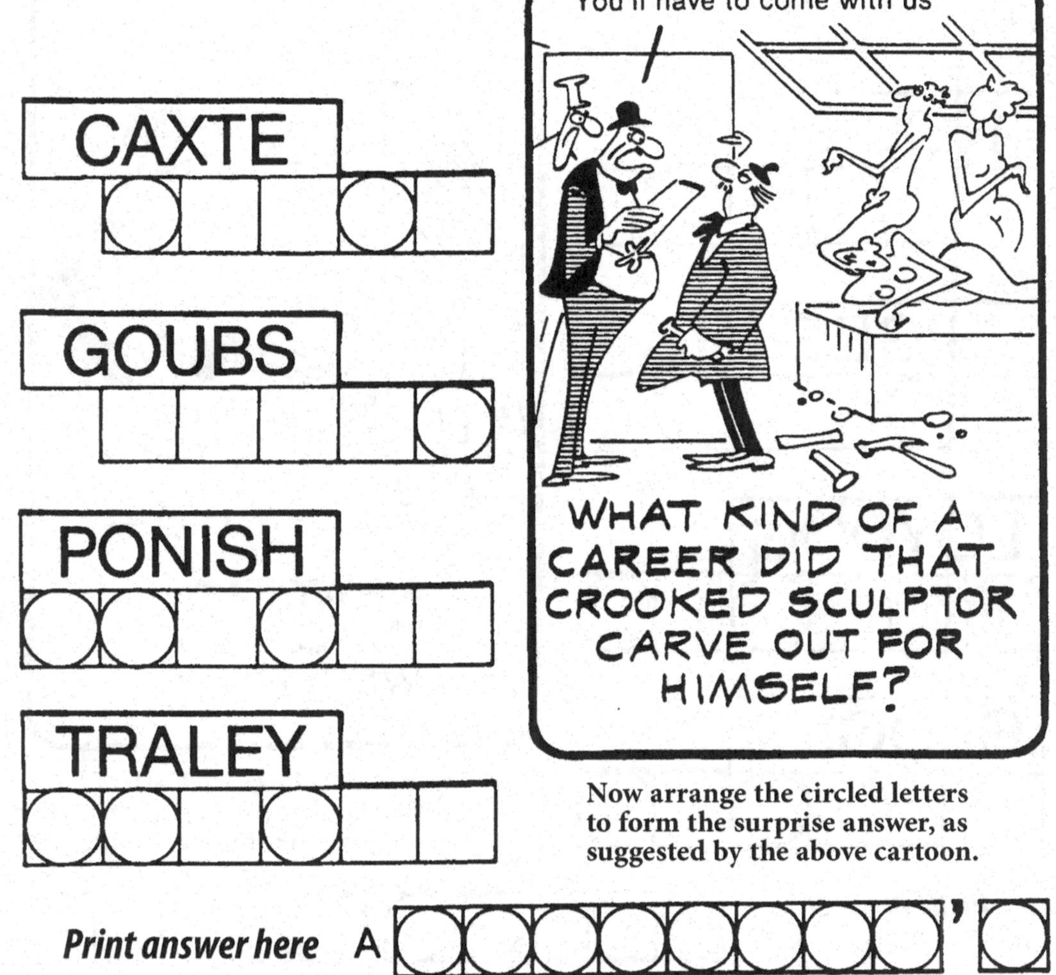

CAXTE
GOUBS
PONISH
TRALEY
You'll have to come with us
WHAT KIND OF A CAREER DID THAT CROOKED SCULPTOR CARVE OUT FOR HIMSELF?

Now arrange the circled letters to form the surprise answer, as suggested by the above cartoon.

Print answer here A ◯◯◯◯◯◯◯◯' ◯

PUZZLE 41

WARNING WARNING WARNING WARNING WARNING WARNING WARNING

JUMBLE®

Unscramble these four Jumbles, one letter to each square, to form four ordinary words.

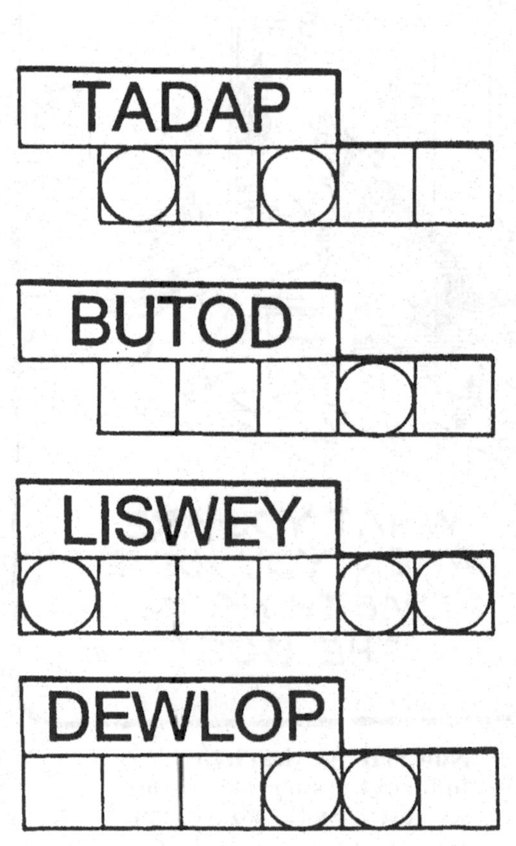

TADAP
BUTOD
LISWEY
DEWLOP

WALL ST.
STOCKS and BONDS
WHAT HAPPENED TO THOSE "PAPER" PROFITS HE SUPPOSEDLY EARNED?

Now arrange the circled letters to form the surprise answer, as suggested by the above cartoon.

Print answer here THEY 

WARNING WARNING WARNING WARNING WARNING WARNING WARNING

JUMBLE®

Unscramble these four Jumbles, one letter to each square, to form four ordinary words.

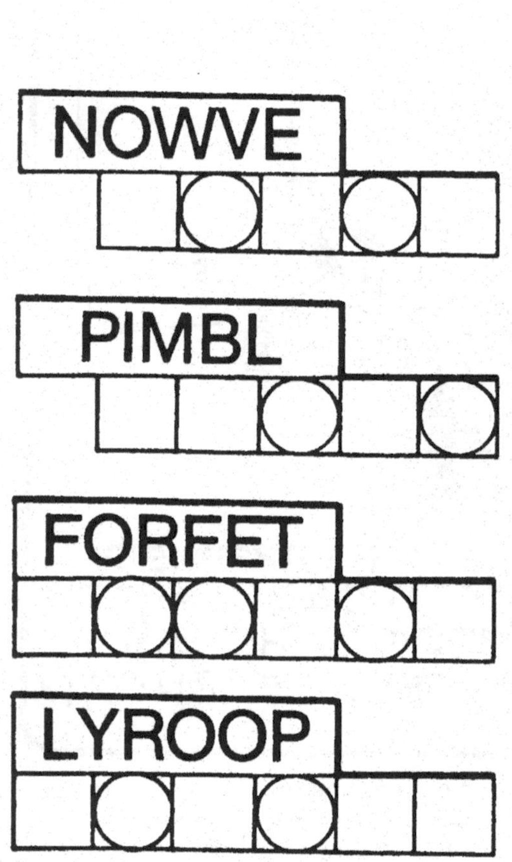
NOWVE
PIMBL
FORFET
LYROOP

This is going to help my career
WHAT YOU ARE WHEN YOU HAVE SOMETHING ON THE BOSS.

Now arrange the circled letters to form the surprise answer, as suggested by the above cartoon.

Print answer here " ◯◯◯◯ ◯◯◯◯◯ "

PUZZLE 43

WARNING WARNING WARNING WARNING WARNING WARNING WARNIN

JUMBLE®

Unscramble these four Jumbles, one letter to each square, to form four ordinary words.

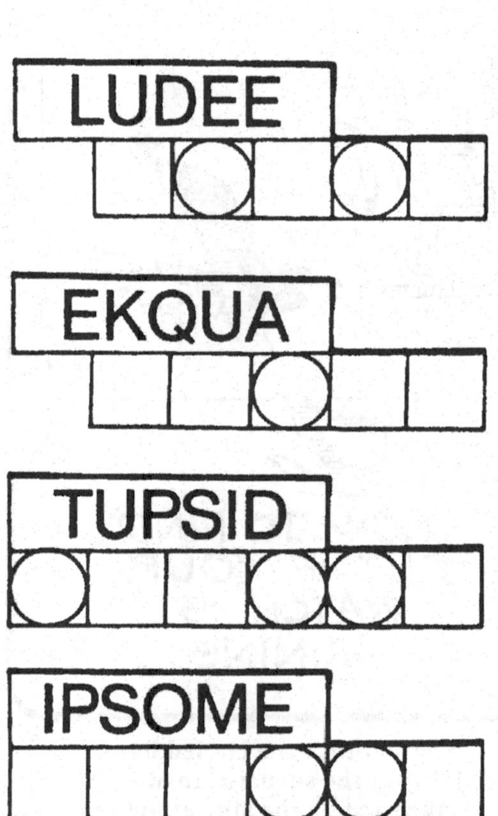
LUDEE
EKQUA
TUPSID
IPSOME

WHAT THE GARBAGEMAN SAID HE WAS.

Now arrange the circled letters to form the surprise answer, as suggested by the above cartoon.

Print answer here AT HER " ______ "

JUMBLE®

Unscramble these four Jumbles, one letter to each square, to form four ordinary words.

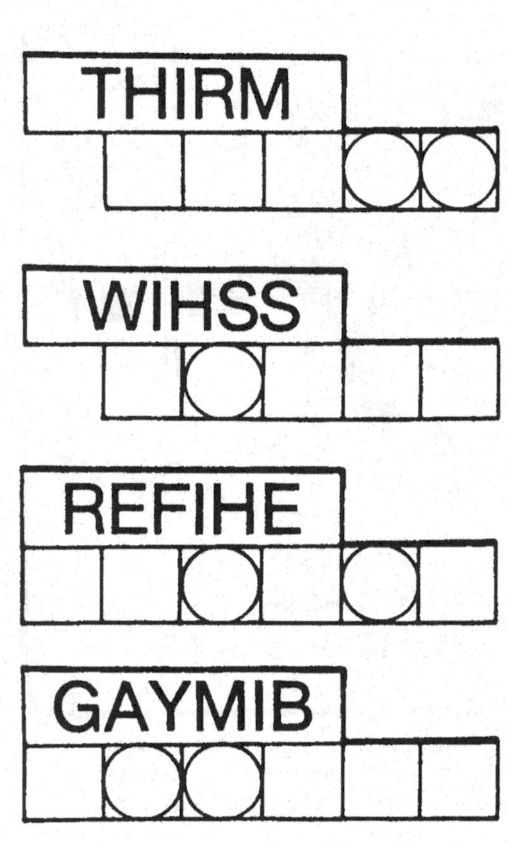

THIRM
WIHSS
REFIHE
GAYMIB

JEWELRY
HOW TO FIND OUT IF YOUR WATCH IS GAINING.

Now arrange the circled letters to form the surprise answer, as suggested by the above cartoon.

Print answer here

PUZZLE 45

WARNING WARNING WARNING WARNING WARNING WARNING WARNING

JUMBLE®

Unscramble these four Jumbles, one letter to each square, to form four ordinary words.

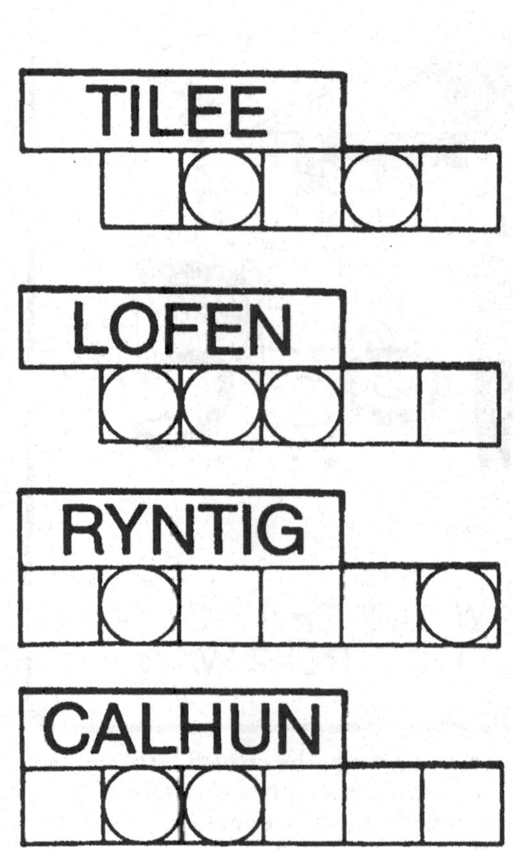
TILEE
LOFEN
RYNTIG
CALHUN

WHEN HE FINALLY GOT THE FIRE-PLACE WORKING, SHE WAS THIS.

Now arrange the circled letters to form the surprise answer, as suggested by the above cartoon.

Print answer here " ◯◯◯◯◯◯ - ◯◯◯◯◯ "

PUZZLE 46

JUMBLE®

Unscramble these four Jumbles, one letter to each square, to form four ordinary words.

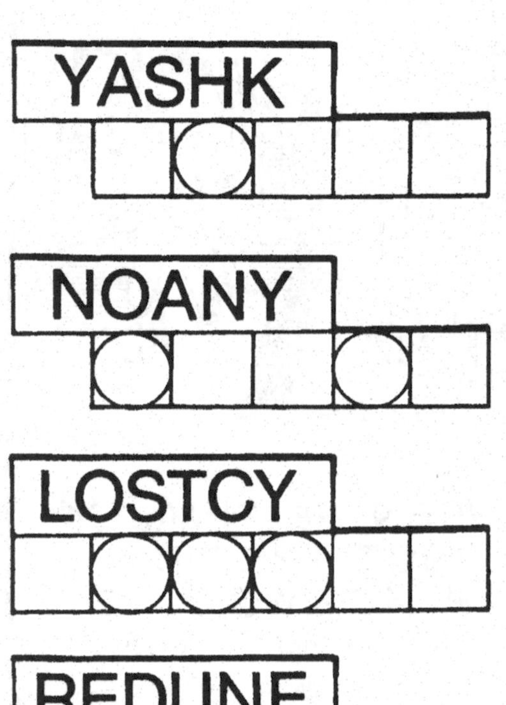

YASHK
NOANY
LOSTCY
REDUNE

Guess I'll have to save up for another one
WHAT THAT OLD HOT ROD WAS.

Now arrange the circled letters to form the surprise answer, as suggested by the above cartoon.

Print answer here

WARNING WARNING WARNING WARNING WARNING WARNING WARNIN

JUMBLE®

Unscramble these four Jumbles, one letter to each square, to form four ordinary words.

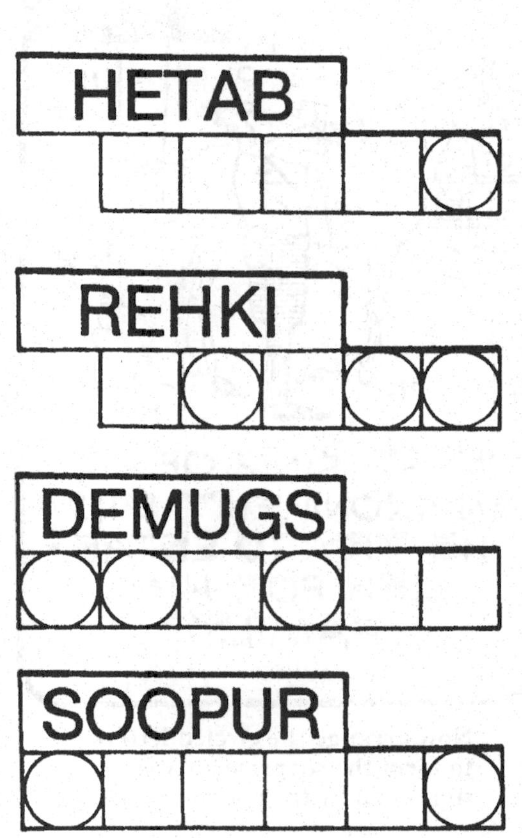
HETAB
REHKI
DEMUGS
SOOPUR

They seem to know what they're doing
WHEN THE COWBOYS FINISHED BRANDING THEM, THE COWS WERE REALLY THIS.

Now arrange the circled letters to form the surprise answer, as suggested by the above cartoon.

Print answer here “”

PUZZLE 48

WARNING WARNING WARNING WARNING WARNING WARNING WARNING

JUMBLE®

Unscramble these four Jumbles, one letter to each square, to form four ordinary words.

VAHEY
LYJOL
SLEENT
ENBOGE
This ought to keep 'em out of trouble
WHAT KIND OF AN ENVIRONMENT DID HE TRY TO ESTAB-LISH FOR HIS FAMILY?
Now arrange the circled letters to form the surprise answer, as suggested by the above cartoon.
Print answer here
A " "

PUZZLE 49

WARNING WARNING WARNING WARNING WARNING WARNING WARNING

JUMBLE®

Unscramble these four Jumbles, one letter to each square, to form four ordinary words.

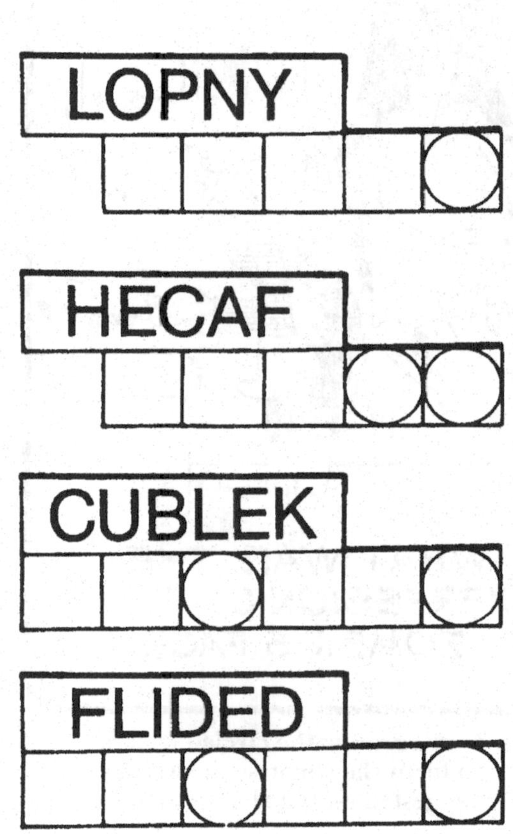

LOPNY
HECAF
CUBLEK
FLIDED

This should keep 'em out
WHAT BARBED WIRE WAS FIRST USED FOR.

Now arrange the circled letters to form the surprise answer, as suggested by the above cartoon.

Print answer here "  "

WARNING WARNING WARNING WARNING WARNING WARNING WARNING

JUMBLE®

Unscramble these four Jumbles, one letter to each square, to form four ordinary words.

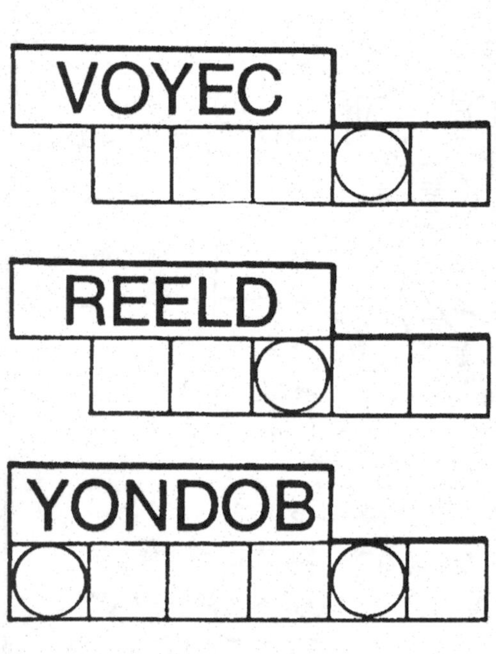
VOYEC
REELD
YONDOB

PALLAP

WHAT WAS THE EXPRESSION ON THAT ZOMBIE'S FACE?

Now arrange the circled letters to form the surprise answer, as suggested by the above cartoon.

Print answer here "   "

PUZZLE
51

WARNING WARNING WARNING WARNING WARNING WARNING WARNIN

JUMBLE®

Unscramble these four Jumbles, one letter to each square, to form four ordinary words.

KLACH
YANER
VANDIE
DUSARI
WHAT HAPPENED TO THE MISSING CAN OF SHELLAC?

Now arrange the circled letters to form the surprise answer, as suggested by the above cartoon.

Print answer here IT " "

PUZZLE 52

JUMBLE®

Unscramble these four Jumbles, one letter to each square, to form four ordinary words.

DUGOH
CALVO
SPELTE
THIMER
3/11
WHAT THE PUP WHO LOVED GETTING WASHED MUST HAVE BEEN.

Now arrange the circled letters to form the surprise answer, as suggested by the above cartoon.

Print answer here A " "

PUZZLE 53

WARNING WARNING WARNING WARNING WARNING WARNING WARNING

JUMBLE®

Unscramble these four Jumbles, one letter to each square, to form four ordinary words.

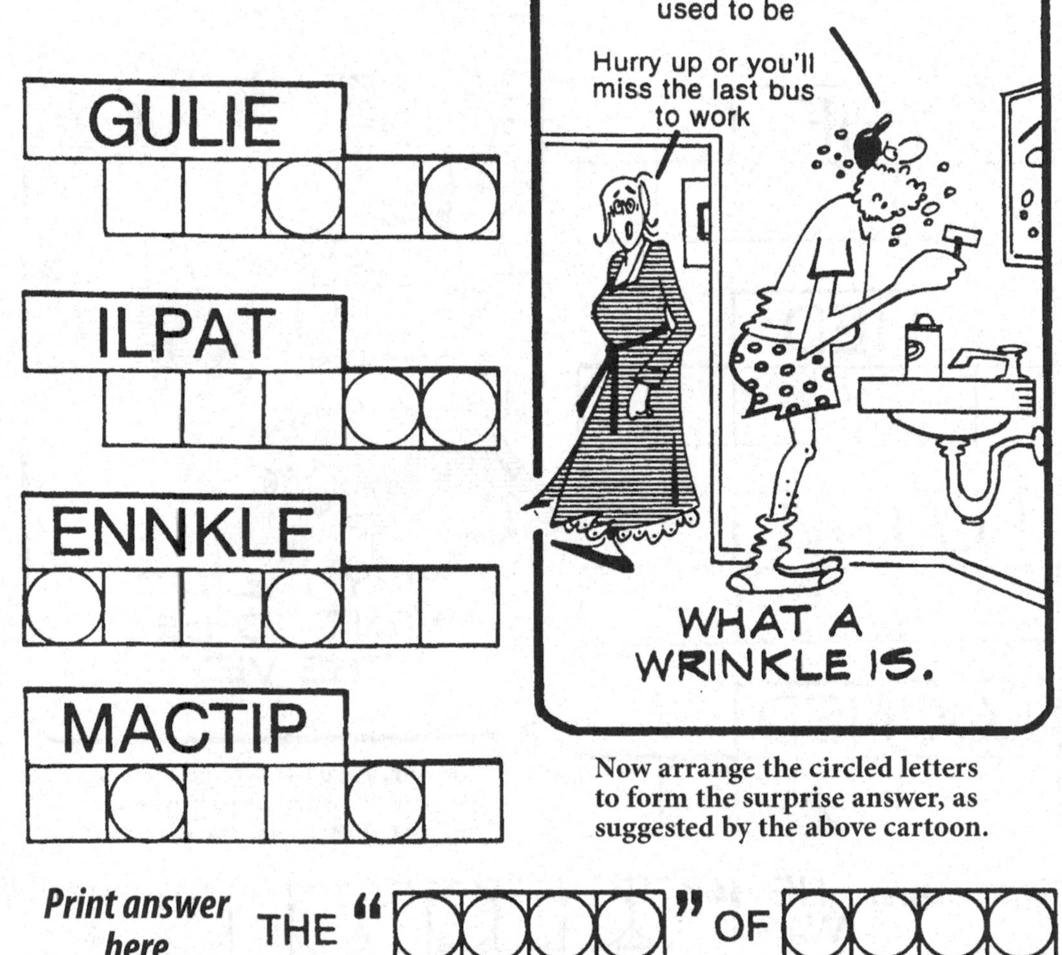

GULIE
ILPAT
ENNKLE
MACTIP
I'm not as young as I used to be
Hurry up or you'll miss the last bus to work
WHAT A WRINKLE IS.

Now arrange the circled letters to form the surprise answer, as suggested by the above cartoon.

Print answer here THE " " OF

JUMBLE®

Unscramble these four Jumbles, one letter to each square, to form four ordinary words.

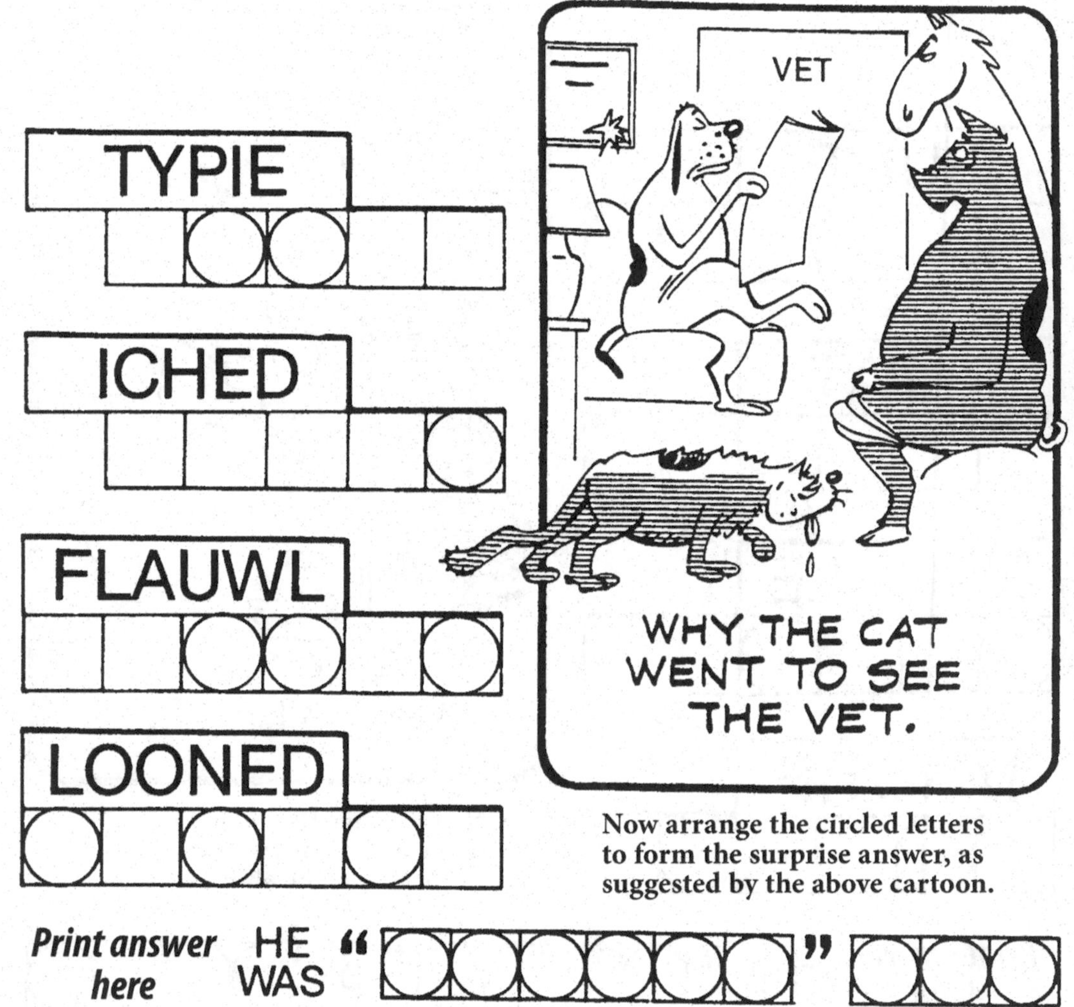
TYPIE
ICHED
FLAUWL
LOONED
VET
WHY THE CAT WENT TO SEE THE VET.

Now arrange the circled letters to form the surprise answer, as suggested by the above cartoon.

Print answer here HE WAS "◯◯◯◯◯◯◯" ◯◯◯

WARNING WARNING WARNING WARNING WARNING WARNING WARNING

JUMBLE®

Unscramble these four Jumbles, one letter to each square, to form four ordinary words.

NAGME
RADIC
UNBOTT
SENCHO
$
WHY THE INVENTOR OF FISHHOOKS BECAME A MILLIONAIRE.

Now arrange the circled letters to form the surprise answer, as suggested by the above cartoon.

Print answer here THEY REALLY “ ”

PUZZLE 56

WARNING WARNING WARNING WARNING WARNING WARNING WARNING

JUMBLE®

Unscramble these four Jumbles, one letter to each square, to form four ordinary words.

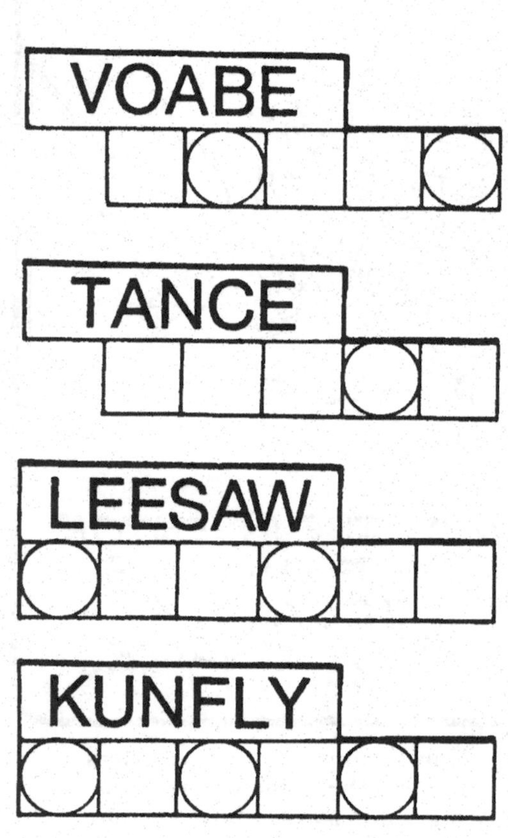
VOABE
TANCE
LEESAW
KUNFLY

They say it pays well
WHAT THE COWBOYS WERE HOPING TO GET OUT OF THE RODEO.

Now arrange the circled letters to form the surprise answer, as suggested by the above cartoon.

Print answer here A

PUZZLE 57

WARNING WARNING WARNING WARNING WARNING WARNING WARNING

JUMBLE®

Unscramble these four Jumbles, one letter to each square, to form four ordinary words.

DEWPI
TANBO
ENTINY
AXALGY
WHAT TO GIVE YOUR WIFE AT 3 A.M.

Now arrange the circled letters to form the surprise answer, as suggested by the above cartoon.

Print answer here AN

WARNING WARNING WARNING WARNING WARNING WARNING WARNING

PUZZLE 58

JUMBLE®

Unscramble these four Jumbles, one letter to each square, to form four ordinary words.

POCHE

DUGAR

STABEK

ACCUST

Don't worry—I'm using red golf balls
WHAT THE COMPULSIVE GOLFER WAS.

Now arrange the circled letters to form the surprise answer, as suggested by the above cartoon.

Print answer here A " "

WARNING WARNING WARNING WARNING WARNING WARNING WARNING

JUMBLE®

Unscramble these four Jumbles, one letter to each square, to form four ordinary words.

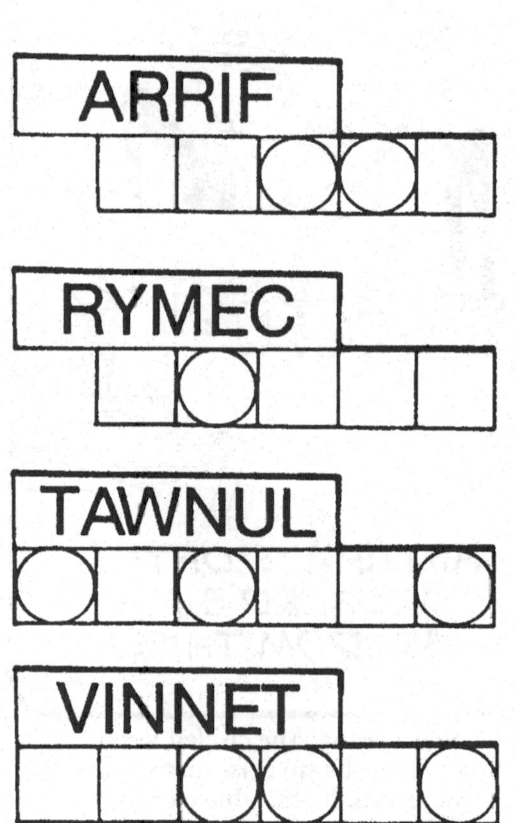
ARRIF
RYMEC
TAWNUL
VINNET

THAT EXECUTIVE SHAKE-UP AMOUNTED TO THIS.

Now arrange the circled letters to form the surprise answer, as suggested by the above cartoon.

Print answer here A "□□□□□" □□□□□

PUZZLE 60

JUMBLE®

Unscramble these four Jumbles, one letter to each square, to form four ordinary words.

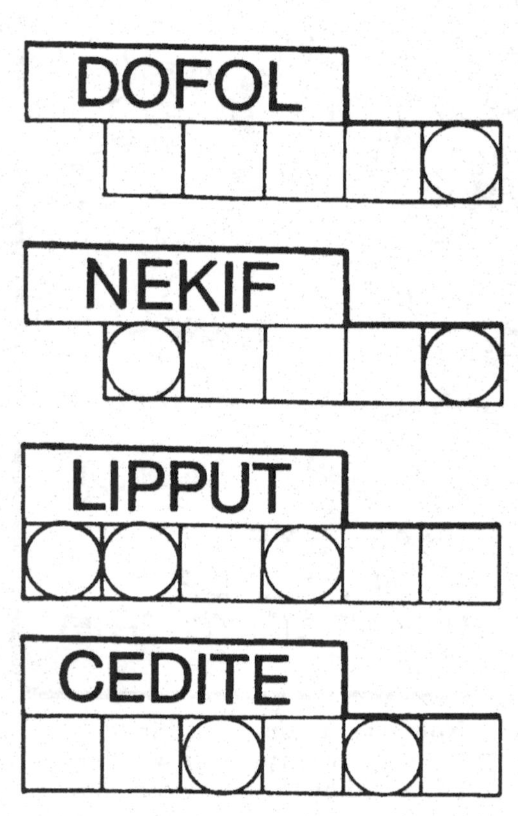
DOFOL
NEKIF
LIPPUT
CEDITE

Some lovely motels in this area
HINTS ARE OFTEN DROPPED BUT SELDOM THIS.

Now arrange the circled letters to form the surprise answer, as suggested by the above cartoon.

Print answer here

PUZZLE 61

WARNING WARNING WARNING WARNING WARNING WARNING WARNING

JUMBLE®

Unscramble these four Jumbles, one letter to each square, to form four ordinary words.

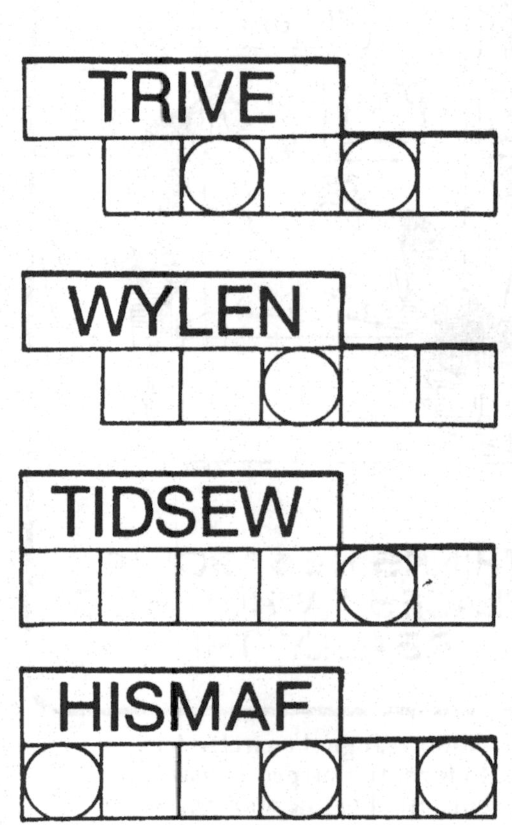
TRIVE
WYLEN
TIDSEW
HISMAF

P.D.
ONE WAY
HE COMMITTED A TRAFFIC VIOLATION WHEN HE WAS DRIVING UNDER THE INFLUENCE OF THIS.

Now arrange the circled letters to form the surprise answer, as suggested by the above cartoon.

Print answer here

JUMBLE®

Unscramble these four Jumbles, one letter to each square, to form four ordinary words.

NEEYM
AXORB
TILBEG
MIKOON
SLICKO ENTERPRISES
THINKS HE'S "GOING PLACES," WHEN HE'S REALLY THIS.

Now arrange the circled letters to form the surprise answer, as suggested by the above cartoon.

Print answer here "   "

PUZZLE 63

WARNING WARNING WARNING WARNING WARNING WARNING WARNING

JUMBLE®

Unscramble these four Jumbles, one letter to each square, to form four ordinary words.

VEROL
YUCIJ
IGGLOO
FONTIY
WHAT THAT SHORT GUY SAID WHILE PROPOSING.
Now arrange the circled letters to form the surprise answer, as suggested by the above cartoon.
Print answer here
" " FOR

WARNING WARNING WARNING WARNING WARNING WARNING WARNING

JUMBLE®

Unscramble these four Jumbles, one letter to each square, to form four ordinary words.

AFMEL
BILLE
KITSCY
SNORPE
Why are their sandwiches so popular?
Word of mouth
DELIC
WHAT YOU'D EXPECT A GOOD TONGUE SANDWICH TO DO.

Now arrange the circled letters to form the surprise answer, as suggested by the above cartoon.

Print answer here FOR

WARNING WARNING WARNING WARNING WARNING WARNING WARNING

JUMBLE®

Unscramble these four Jumbles, one letter to each square, to form four ordinary words.

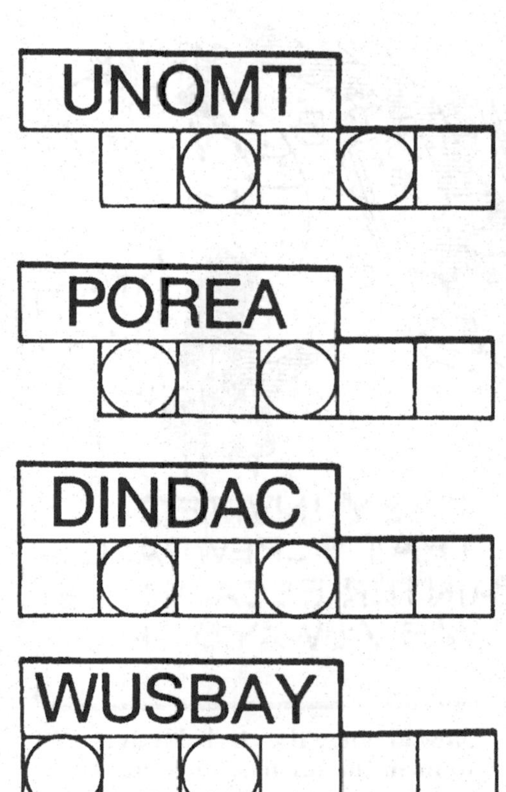
UNOMT
POREA
DINDAC
WUSBAY

WHAT HE SAID WHEN THE JUDGE SENTENCED HIM TO BE HANGED.

Now arrange the circled letters to form the surprise answer, as suggested by the above cartoon.

Print answer here THAT'S ◯◯◯ "◯◯◯◯◯"

JUMBLE®

Unscramble these four Jumbles, one letter to each square, to form four ordinary words.

FRADT
YONEH
YIRCKT
LAWSUR
This'll blow your mind!
THEY INVITED THAT SCREWBALL PAINTER BECAUSE HE WAS ALWAYS THIS.

Now arrange the circled letters to form the surprise answer, as suggested by the above cartoon.

Print answer here THE ◯◯◯◯ OF THE "◯◯◯◯"

PUZZLE
67

WARNING WARNING WARNING WARNING WARNING WARNING WARNING

JUMBLE®

Unscramble these four Jumbles, one letter to each square, to form four ordinary words.

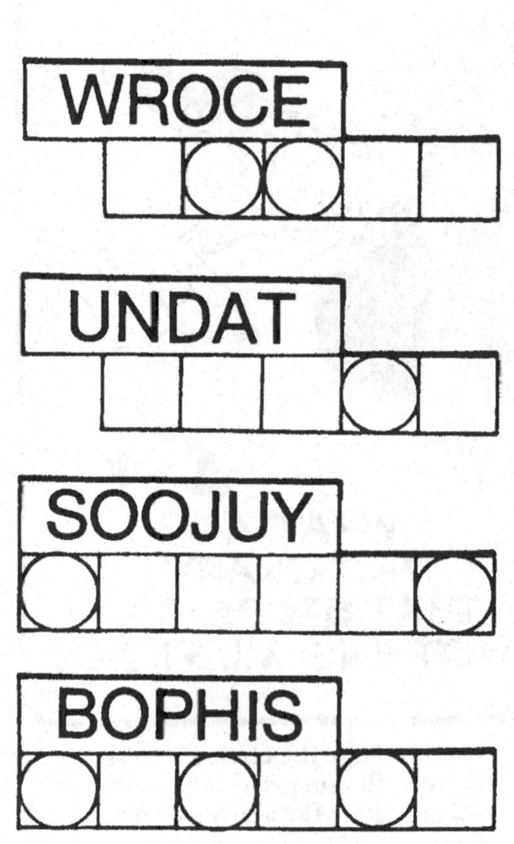

WROCE
UNDAT
SOOJUY
BOPHIS

I'm fast and cheap!
HE KNEW HOW TO MAKE EXTRA MONEY WITH HIS SHOVEL BY BEING GOOD AT THIS.

Now arrange the circled letters to form the surprise answer, as suggested by the above cartoon.

Print answer here

PUZZLE 68

WARNING WARNING WARNING WARNING WARNING WARNING WARNING

JUMBLE®

Unscramble these four Jumbles, one letter to each square, to form four ordinary words.

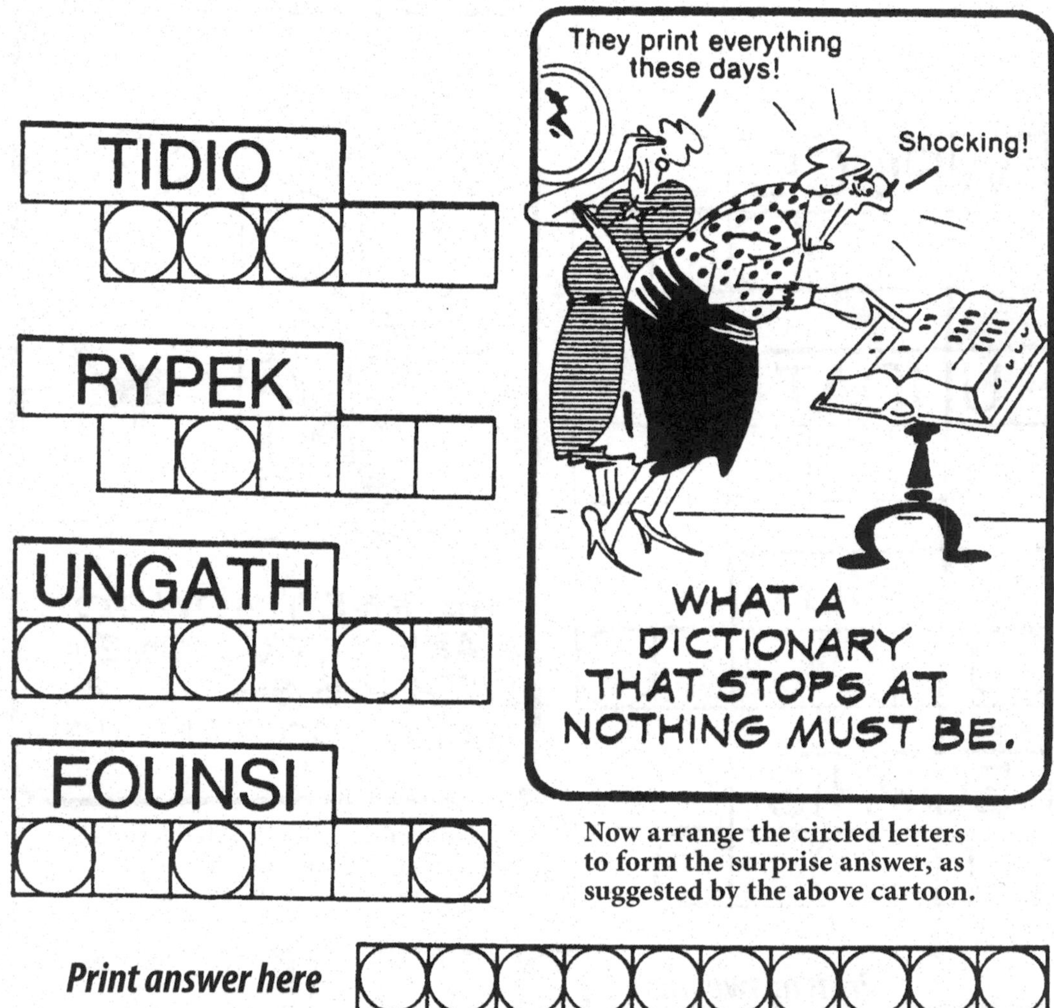

TIDIO
RYPEK
UNGATH
FOUNSI
They print everything these days!
Shocking!
WHAT A DICTIONARY THAT STOPS AT NOTHING MUST BE.

Now arrange the circled letters to form the surprise answer, as suggested by the above cartoon.

Print answer here

PUZZLE 69

WARNING WARNING WARNING WARNING WARNING WARNING WARNING

JUMBLE®

Unscramble these four Jumbles, one letter to each square, to form four ordinary words.

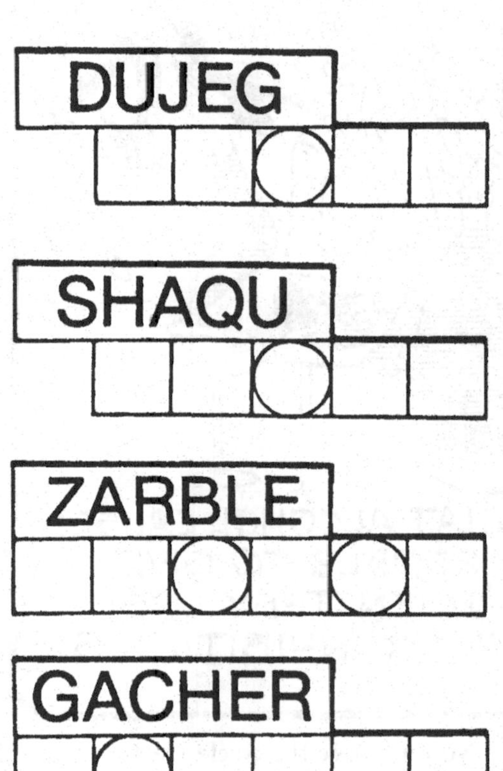

DUJEG
SHAQU
ZARBLE
GACHER

He's sure got what it takes!
SOMETHING YOU GET BY USING IT.

Now arrange the circled letters to form the surprise answer, as suggested by the above cartoon.

Print answer here

WARNING WARNING WARNING WARNING WARNING WARNING WARNING

JUMBLE®

Unscramble these four Jumbles, one letter to each square, to form four ordinary words.

WHAT ALCOHOL CAUSES PEOPLE TO GIVE WHEN THEY LOSE THEIR INHIBITIONS.

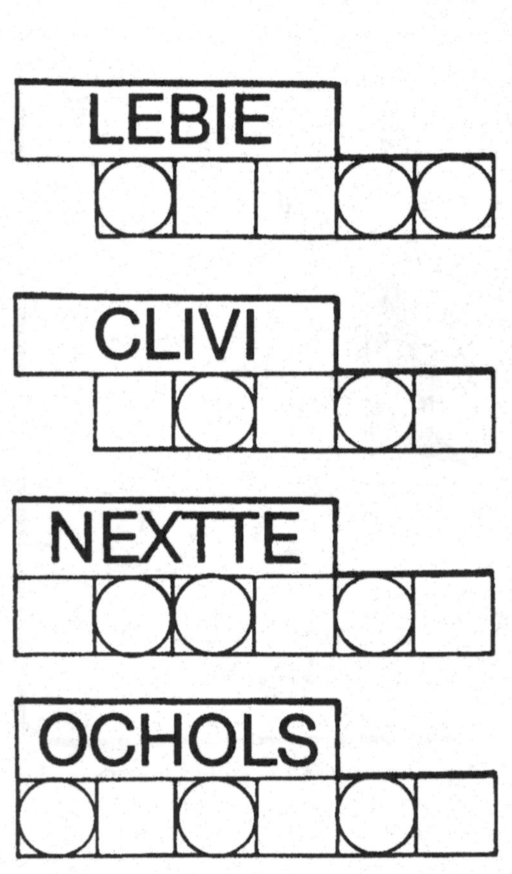
LEBIE
CLIVI
NEXTTE
OCHOLS

Now arrange the circled letters to form the surprise answer, as suggested by the above cartoon.

Print answer here

PUZZLE 71

WARNING WARNING WARNING WARNING WARNING WARNING WARNING

JUMBLE®

Unscramble these four Jumbles, one letter to each square, to form four ordinary words.

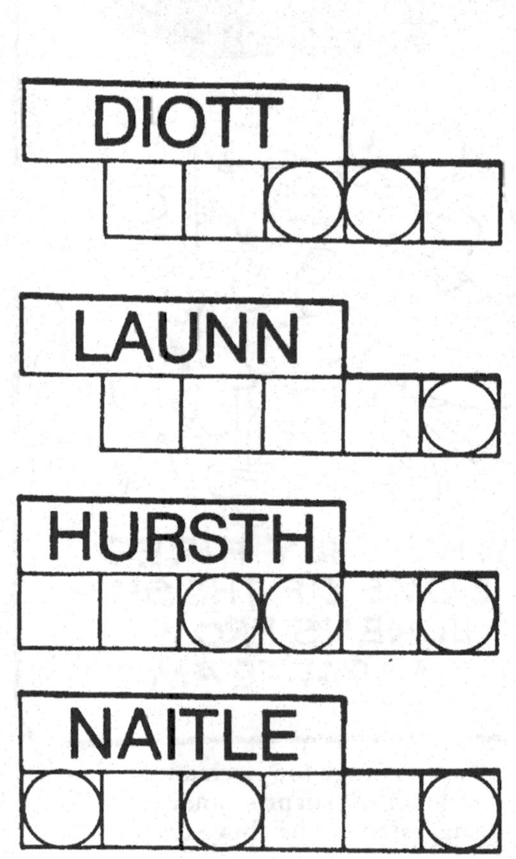

DIOTT
LAUNN
HURSTH
NAITLE

What do you think of our new furniture?
A little tacky
Shh!
"TACT" IS WHAT SOME PEOPLE HAVE WHILE OTHERS DO THIS.

Now arrange the circled letters to form the surprise answer, as suggested by the above cartoon.

Print answer here  THE 

WARNING WARNING WARNING WARNING WARNING WARNING WARNING

JUMBLE®

Unscramble these four Jumbles, one letter to each square, to form four ordinary words.

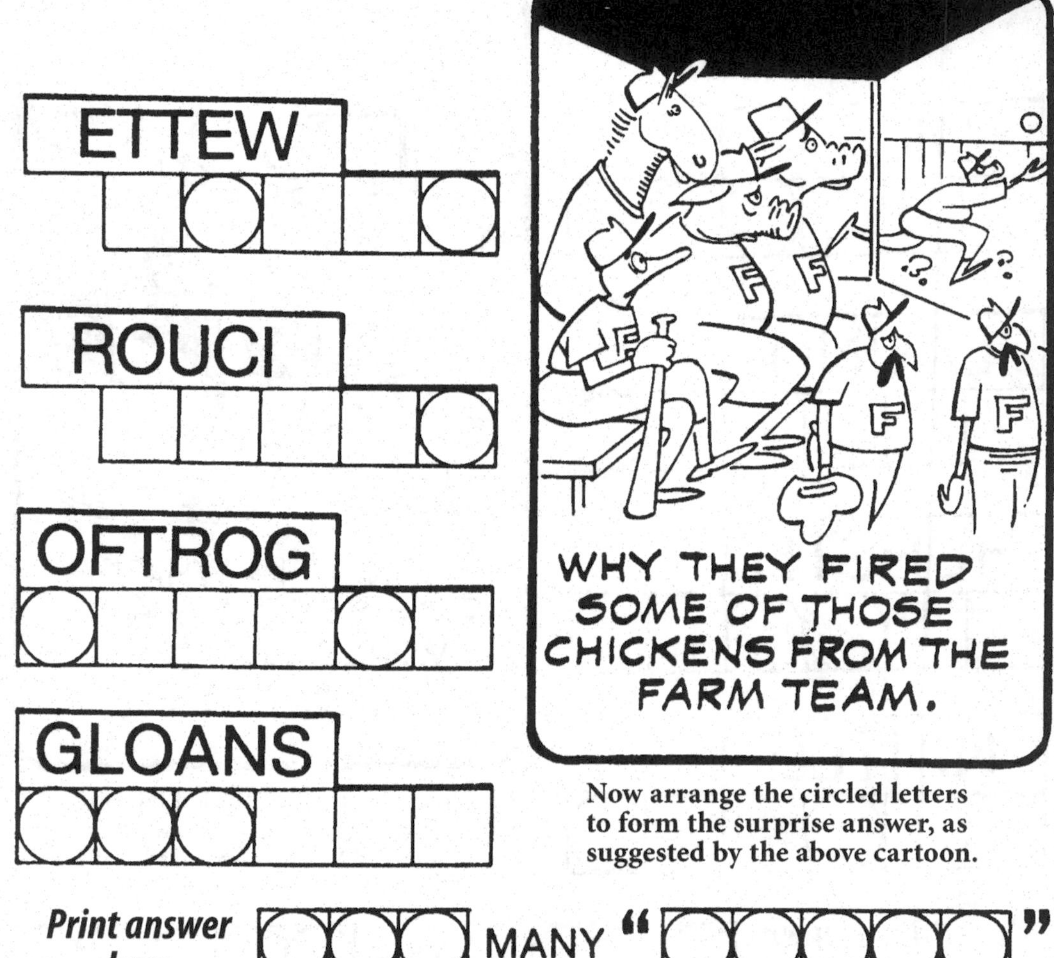
ETTEW
ROUCI
OFTROG
GLOANS
WHY THEY FIRED SOME OF THOSE CHICKENS FROM THE FARM TEAM.

Now arrange the circled letters to form the surprise answer, as suggested by the above cartoon.

Print answer here ◯◯◯ MANY "◯◯◯◯◯"

PUZZLE 73

WARNING WARNING WARNING WARNING WARNING WARNING WARNING

JUMBLE®

Unscramble these four Jumbles, one letter to each square, to form four ordinary words.

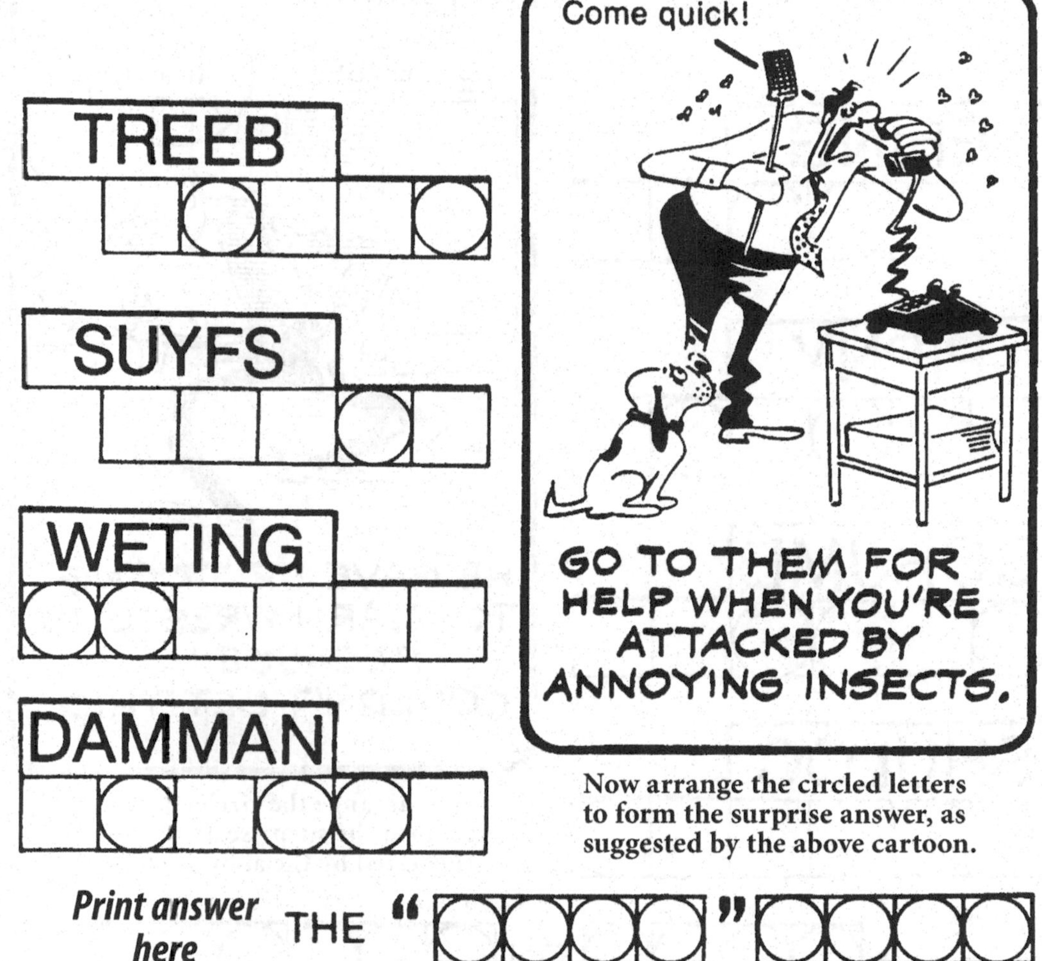
TREEB
SUYFS
WETING
DAMMAN
Come quick!
GO TO THEM FOR HELP WHEN YOU'RE ATTACKED BY ANNOYING INSECTS.

Now arrange the circled letters to form the surprise answer, as suggested by the above cartoon.

Print answer here THE "◯◯◯◯◯" ◯◯◯◯◯

WARNING WARNING WARNING WARNING WARNING WARNING WARNING

JUMBLE®

Unscramble these four Jumbles, one letter to each square, to form four ordinary words.

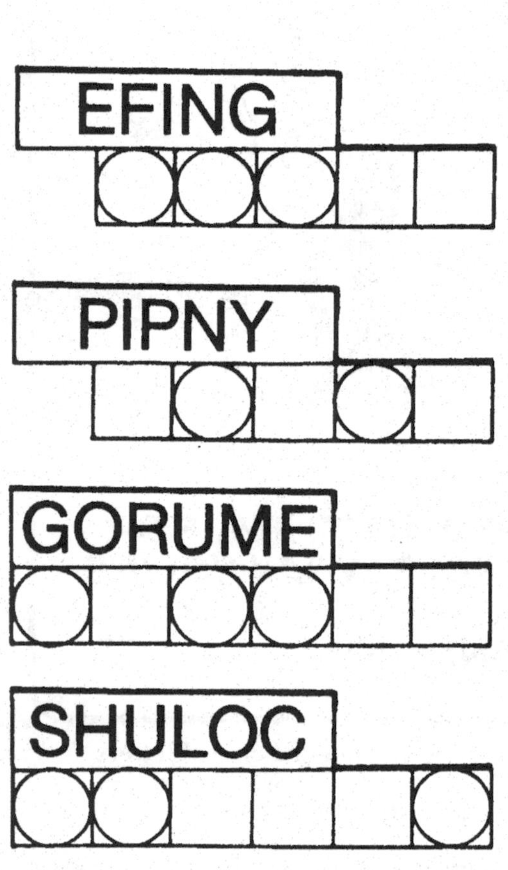
EFING
PIPNY
GORUME
SHULOC

LEARN SELF-DEFENSE
I can't take it anymore
HE GAVE UP TRYING TO LEARN WRESTLING BECAUSE HE COULDN'T GET THIS.

Now arrange the circled letters to form the surprise answer, as suggested by the above cartoon.

Print answer here A ○○○○ ON ○○○○○○○

WARNING WARNING WARNING WARNING WARNING WARNING WARNING

JUMBLE®

Unscramble these four Jumbles, one letter to each square, to form four ordinary words.

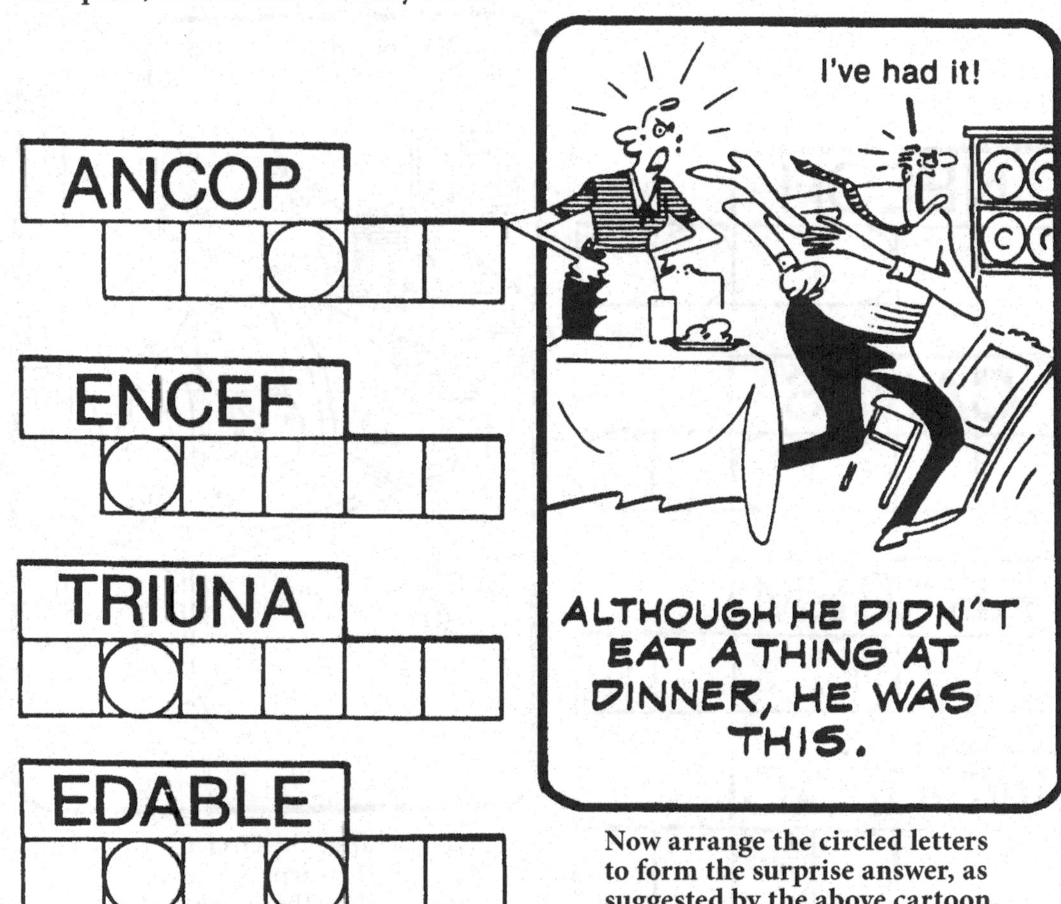

ANCOP
ENCEF
TRIUNA
EDABLE
I've had it!
ALTHOUGH HE DIDN'T EAT A THING AT DINNER, HE WAS THIS.

Now arrange the circled letters to form the surprise answer, as suggested by the above cartoon.

Print answer here “”

JUMBLE®

Unscramble these four Jumbles, one letter to each square, to form four ordinary words.

NEECH
CANKS
KRABEM
WORDAC
WHEN DID YOU FIRST NOTICE THAT WEAK BACK?

Now arrange the circled letters to form the surprise answer, as suggested by the above cartoon.

Print answer here “ ”

WARNING WARNING WARNING WARNING WARNING WARNING WARNING

JUMBLE®

Unscramble these four Jumbles, one letter to each square, to form four ordinary words.

SUROE
MEFAD
GOCHUR
KOYDEN
You're fired!
Who cares?
THE BAKER LEFT HIS JOB BECAUSE HE DIDN'T THIS.

Now arrange the circled letters to form the surprise answer, as suggested by the above cartoon.

Print answer here " " THE

JUMBLE®

Unscramble these four Jumbles, one letter to each square, to form four ordinary words.

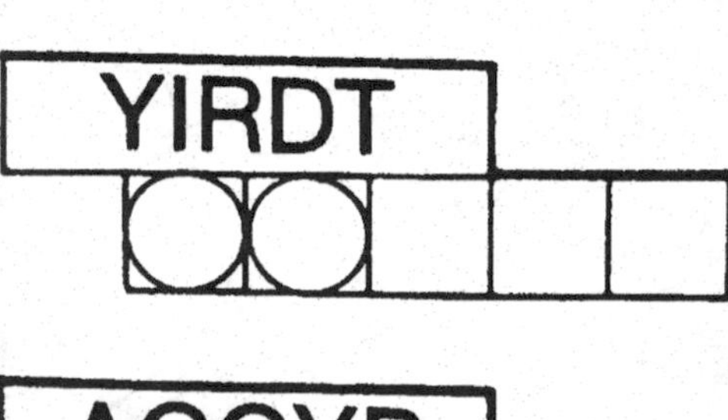
YIRDT

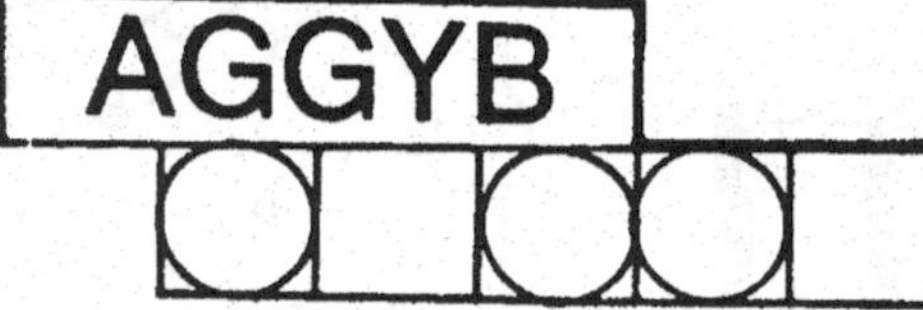
AGGYB

DEDUIG

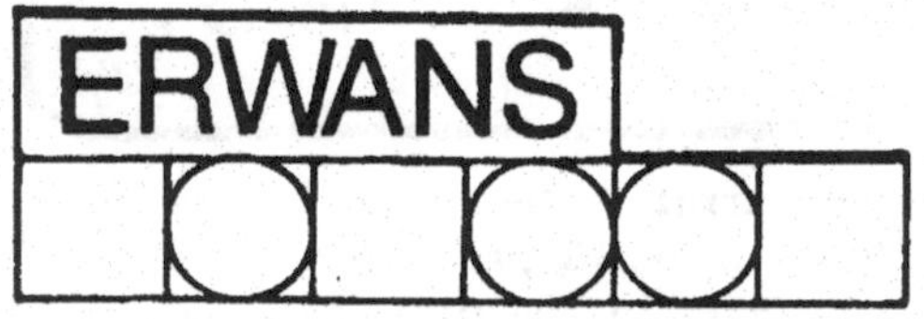
ERWANS

WHAT DO YOU GET
WHEN A FAT MAN
MARRIES A FAT
LADY?

Now arrange the circled letters to form the surprise answer, as suggested by the above cartoon.

Print answer here

A

PUZZLE 79

WARNING WARNING WARNING WARNING WARNING WARNING WARNING

JUMBLE®

Unscramble these four Jumbles, one letter to each square, to form four ordinary words.

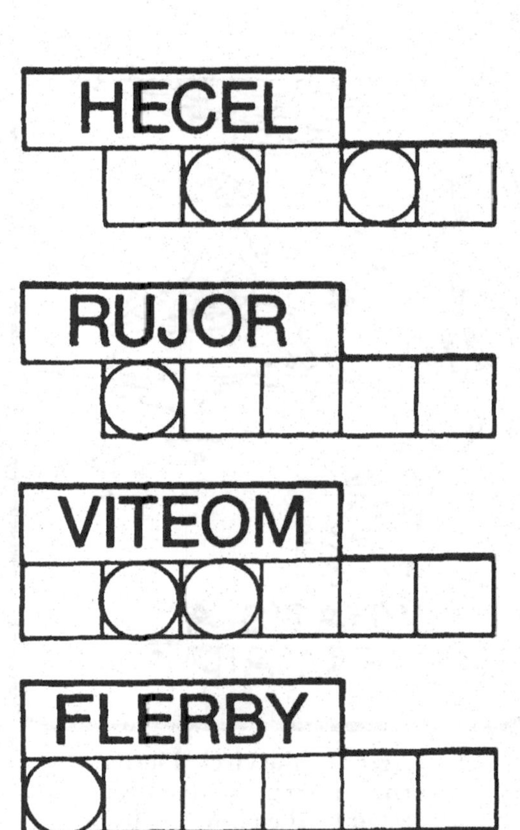
HECEL
RUJOR
VITEOM
FLERBY

WHAT YOU MIGHT EXPECT HIM TO DO WHEN SHE SPENDS ALL THAT MONEY ON SOME SILLY ART OBJECT.

Now arrange the circled letters to form the surprise answer, as suggested by the above cartoon.

Print answer here 

WARNING WARNING WARNING WARNING WARNING WARNING WARNING

JUMBLE®

Unscramble these four Jumbles, one letter to each square, to form four ordinary words.

SIPOE
TIHHC
MIESED
YUFEEL
WHAT'S A MERMAID?
Print answer here
A " - "

Now arrange the circled letters to form the surprise answer, as suggested by the above cartoon.

PUZZLE 81

JUMBLE®

Unscramble these four Jumbles, one letter to each square, to form four ordinary words.

TIGZL
LIGRL
NHETCR
TALTET
Changing from a four-way stop will help relieve congestion.
I think we'll all agree to do this.
THEY WANTED TO INSTALL A NEW TRAFFIC SIGNAL AND JUST NEEDED THE CITY TO ---

Now arrange the circled letters to form the surprise answer, as suggested by the above cartoon.

Print answer here

PUZZLE 82

WARNING WARNING WARNING WARNING WARNING WARNING WARNING

JUMBLE®

Unscramble these four Jumbles, one letter to each square, to form four ordinary words.

OZAKO

LNIBK

TRUCCH

PLWARS

Why have we stopped?
We're out of rails! We can only lay ties until we get more.
CONSTRUCTION OF THE RAILROAD WOULD FALL BEHIND SCHEDULE IF THEY DIDN'T GET ---

Now arrange the circled letters to form the surprise answer, as suggested by the above cartoon.

Print answer here

PUZZLE 83

WARNING WARNING WARNING WARNING WARNING WARNING WARNING

JUMBLE®

Unscramble these four Jumbles, one letter to each square, to form four ordinary words.

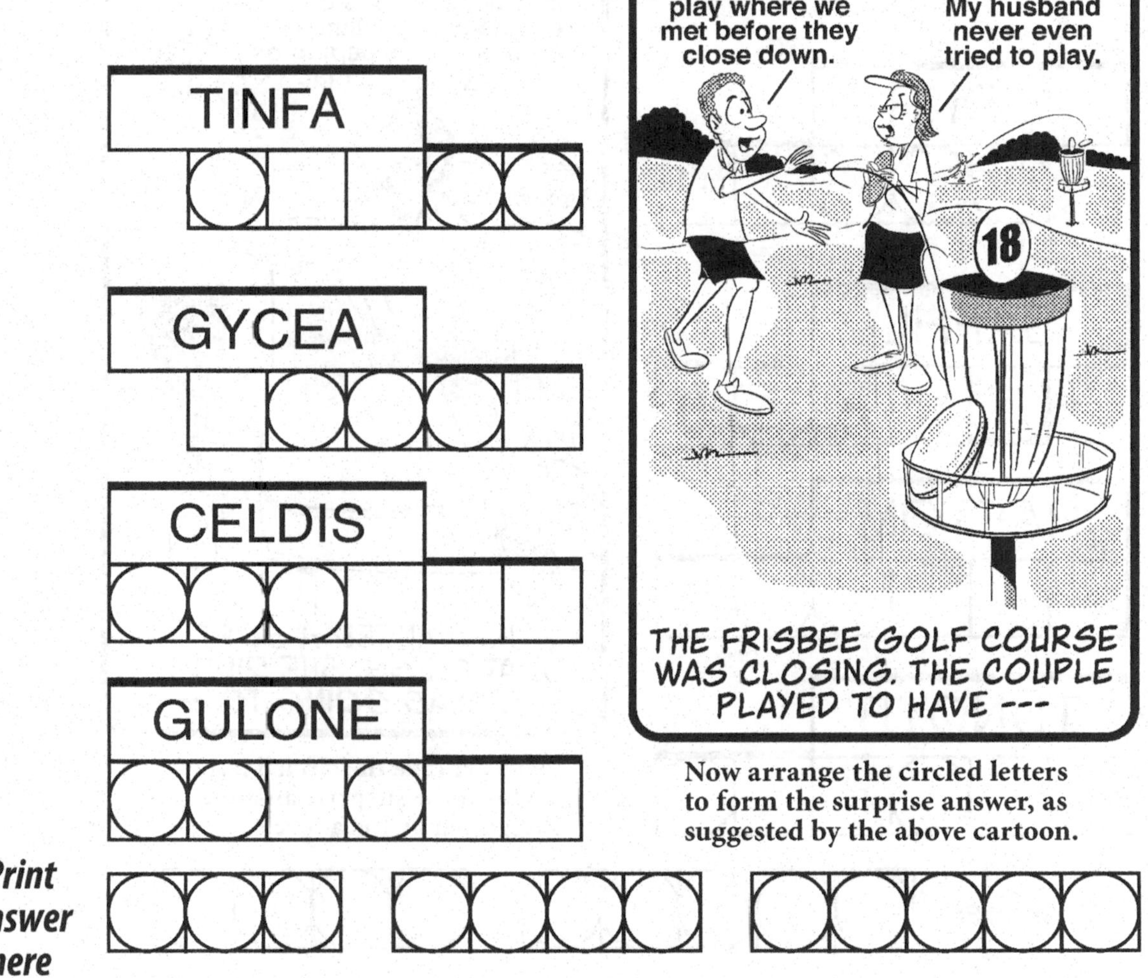
TINFA
GYCEA
CELDIS
GULONE
At least we get to play where we met before they close down.
My husband never even tried to play.
18
THE FRISBEE GOLF COURSE WAS CLOSING. THE COUPLE PLAYED TO HAVE ---

Now arrange the circled letters to form the surprise answer, as suggested by the above cartoon.

Print answer here

PUZZLE 84

WARNING WARNING WARNING WARNING WARNING WARNING WARNING

JUMBLE®

Unscramble these four Jumbles, one letter to each square, to form four ordinary words.

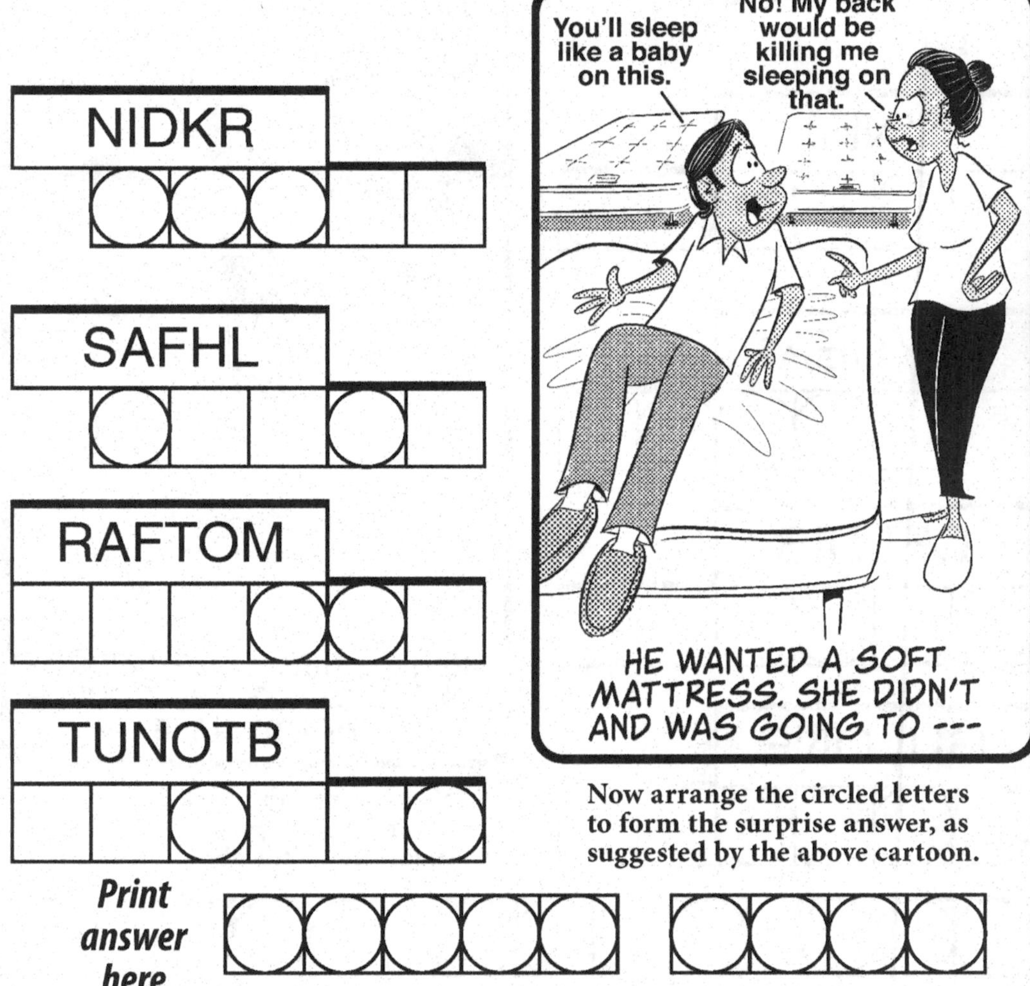
NIDKR
SAFHL
RAFTOM
TUNOTB
You'll sleep like a baby on this.
No! My back would be killing me sleeping on that.
HE WANTED A SOFT MATTRESS. SHE DIDN'T AND WAS GOING TO ---
Now arrange the circled letters to form the surprise answer, as suggested by the above cartoon.
Print answer here

PUZZLE
85

WARNING WARNING WARNING WARNING WARNING WARNING WARNING

JUMBLE®

Unscramble these four Jumbles, one letter to each square, to form four ordinary words.

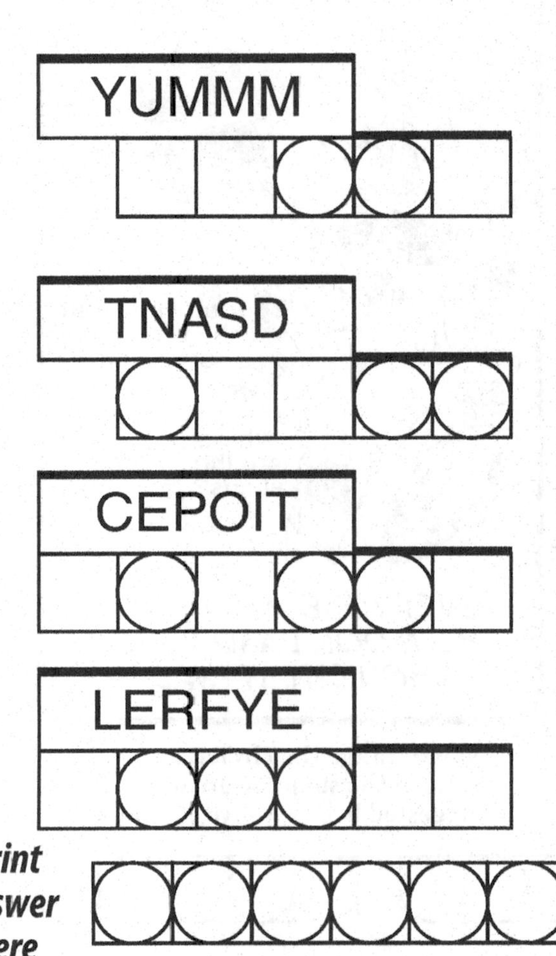

YUMMM
TNASD
CEPOIT
LERFYE
Print answer here

Here, you can see the clock's evolution.
We've come a long way.
My watch can tell me the weather.
12:00
CLOCKS DIDN'T GO DIGITAL UNTIL ---

Now arrange the circled letters to form the surprise answer, as suggested by the above cartoon.

WARNING WARNING WARNING WARNING WARNING WARNING WARNING

JUMBLE®

Unscramble these four Jumbles, one letter to each square, to form four ordinary words.

LIYOD
WFERE
ROHDUS
OAMTOT
Laura, Jeff, you kids are watching history.
Can I look out the window to see them?
Where are the aliens?
EVERYONE WHO SAW THE MOON LANDING ON TV THOUGHT IT WAS ---

Now arrange the circled letters to form the surprise answer, as suggested by the above cartoon.

Print answer here

PUZZLE 87

WARNING WARNING WARNING WARNING WARNING WARNING WARNING

JUMBLE®

Unscramble these four Jumbles, one letter to each square, to form four ordinary words.

GELUN

EGIRT

CONPOH

HACCEN

I don't think we're going to have much to sell for Halloween.
We'll get through this.
BECAUSE OF A DROUGHT, THE PUMPKIN FARMERS WERE GOING THROUGH A ---

Now arrange the circled letters to form the surprise answer, as suggested by the above cartoon.

Print answer here

WARNING WARNING WARNING WARNING WARNING WARNING WARNING

JUMBLE®

Unscramble these four Jumbles, one letter to each square, to form four ordinary words.

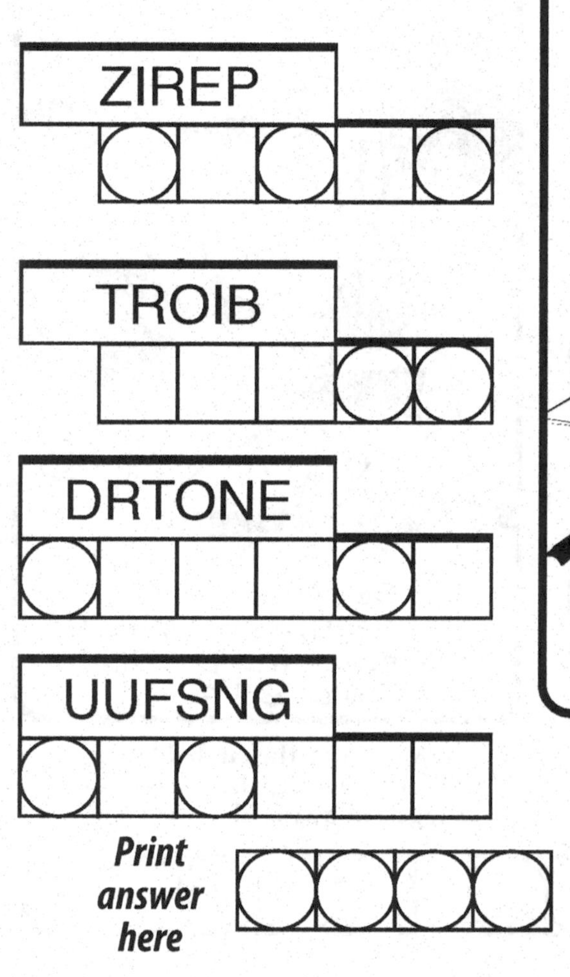
ZIREP
TROIB
DRTONE
UUFSNG

I told you we had to pay today.
It says that we even have to pay on holidays. I didn't know that.
THEY'D GOTTEN A $70 PARKING TICKET, AND NOW HE WAS READING THE ---

Now arrange the circled letters to form the surprise answer, as suggested by the above cartoon.

Print answer here

PUZZLE 89

WARNING WARNING WARNING WARNING WARNING WARNING WARNING

JUMBLE®

Unscramble these four Jumbles, one letter to each square, to form four ordinary words.

LISAA
NURTE
NACITT
OTTUMS
Hey! Keep it down, will ya?
I can hear every word you're saying. You keep it down.
THE CAMPSITES BEING SMALLER THAN EXPECTED RESULTED IN A ---

Now arrange the circled letters to form the surprise answer, as suggested by the above cartoon.

Print answer here

PUZZLE 90

WARNING WARNING WARNING WARNING WARNING WARNING WARNING

JUMBLE®

Unscramble these four Jumbles, one letter to each square, to form four ordinary words.

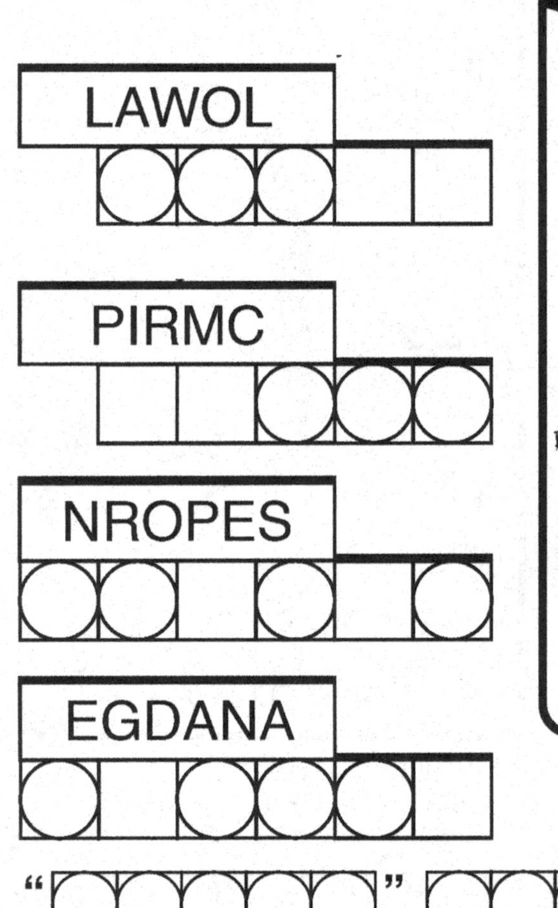

LAWOL
PIRMC
NROPES
EGDANA

If we just get enough speed, it should fly.
What if you put three more propellers on it?
Let's just keep what we have.
THE WRIGHT BROTHERS' APPROACH TO AVIATION WAS ---

Now arrange the circled letters to form the surprise answer, as suggested by the above cartoon.

Print answer here " ○○○○○ " ○○○ ○○○○○○

PUZZLE
91

WARNING WARNING WARNING WARNING WARNING WARNING WARNING

JUMBLE®

Unscramble these four Jumbles, one letter to each square, to form four ordinary words.

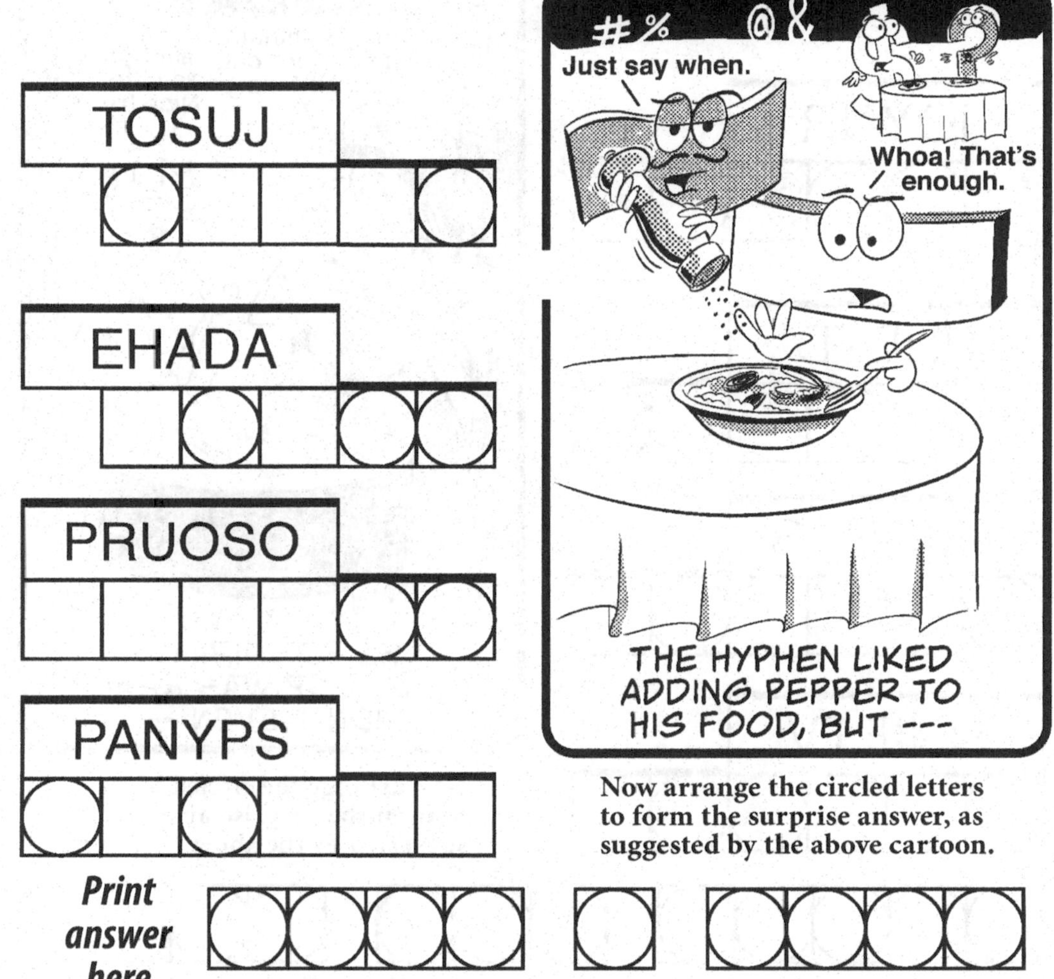
TOSUJ
EHADA
PRUOSO
PANYPS
#% @&
Just say when.
Whoa! That's enough.
THE HYPHEN LIKED ADDING PEPPER TO HIS FOOD, BUT ---
Now arrange the circled letters to form the surprise answer, as suggested by the above cartoon.
Print answer here

WARNING WARNING WARNING WARNING WARNING WARNING WARNING

PUZZLE 92

JUMBLE®

Unscramble these four Jumbles, one letter to each square, to form four ordinary words.

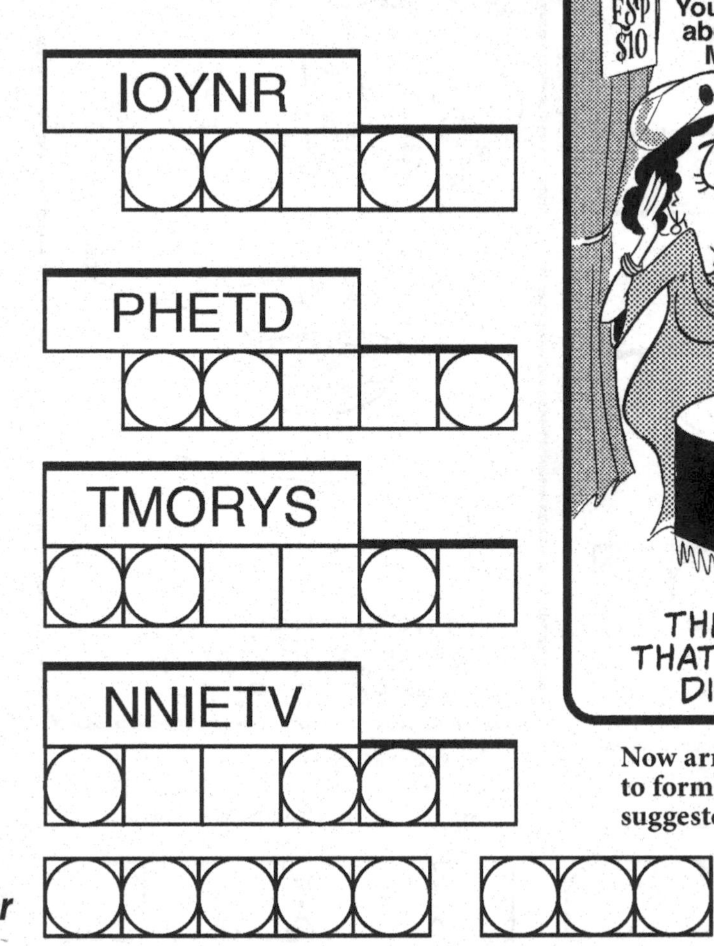

IOYNR
PHETD
TMORYS
NNIETV

ESP $10
You are thinking about your cat, Mr. Mittens.
I'm allergic to cats. Nice try.
THE POSSIBILITY THAT ESP WAS REAL DIDN'T EVEN --

Now arrange the circled letters to form the surprise answer, as suggested by the above cartoon.

Print answer here

PUZZLE 93

WARNING WARNING WARNING WARNING WARNING WARNING WARNING

JUMBLE®

Unscramble these four Jumbles, one letter to each square, to form four ordinary words.

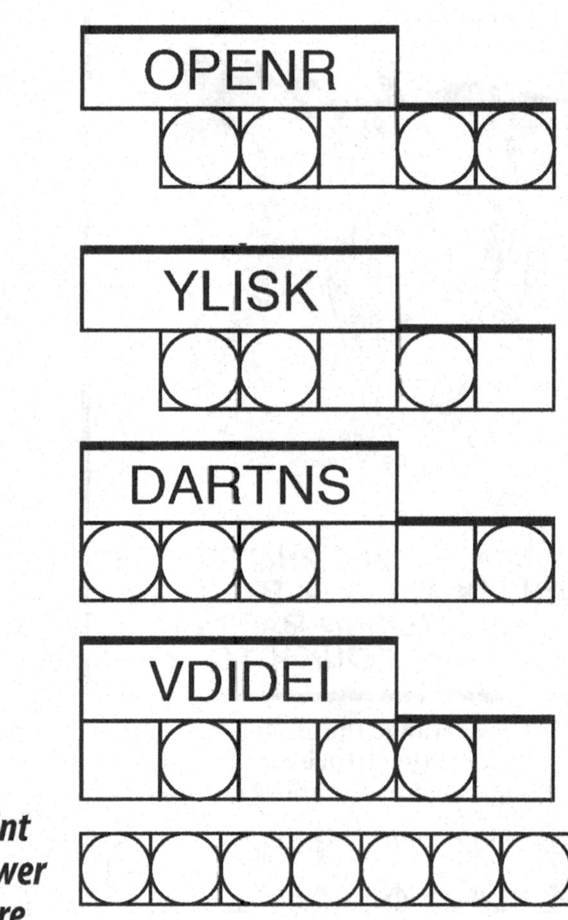

OPENR
YLISK
DARTNS
VDIDEI

I believed there was nothing more rewarding than helping other people.
That's why I became a firefighter too!
THE GHOSTS GOT ALONG SO WELL BECAUSE THEY WERE ---

Now arrange the circled letters to form the surprise answer, as suggested by the above cartoon.

Print answer here

PUZZLE 94

WARNING WARNING WARNING WARNING WARNING WARNING WARNING

JUMBLE®

Unscramble these four Jumbles, one letter to each square, to form four ordinary words.

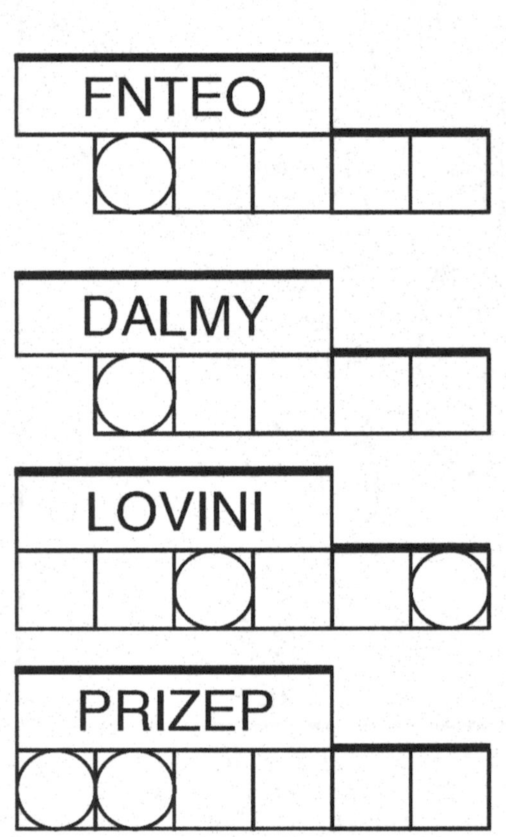

FNTEO
DALMY
LOVINI
PRIZEP

He's just going too fast to catch.
I'm just shooting in wide angle.
WHEN TAKING PHOTOS OF CHUCK YEAGER BREAKING THE SOUND BARRIER, IT WAS TOUGH TO ---

Now arrange the circled letters to form the surprise answer, as suggested by the above cartoon.

Print answer here 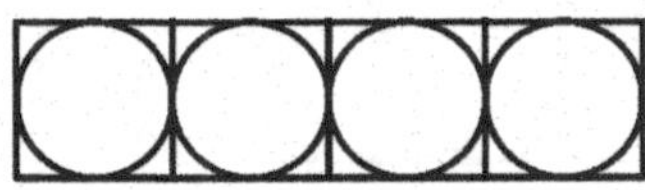 

PUZZLE 95

WARNING WARNING WARNING WARNING WARNING WARNING WARNING

JUMBLE®

Unscramble these four Jumbles, one letter to each square, to form four ordinary words.

KOEEV
VILGI
SLIDAM
GITKNH
It's like a palace!
I can't believe we're here.
WHEN PEOPLE VISIT GRACELAND, THEY GET TO SEE HOW ELVIS ---
Print answer here

Now arrange the circled letters to form the surprise answer, as suggested by the above cartoon.

WARNING WARNING WARNING WARNING WARNING WARNING WARNING

JUMBLE®

Unscramble these four Jumbles, one letter to each square, to form four ordinary words.

CHABE

GUYON

ARYTRO

SFOLYK

I hope all these billboards work.
FAMILY FIX-IT SHOP
We can fix anything!
We've put everything into them.
THE HANDYMAN SPENT SO MUCH ON ADVERTISING BECAUSE HE WANTED TO ---

Now arrange the circled letters to form the surprise answer, as suggested by the above cartoon.

Print answer here

WARNING WARNING WARNING WARNING WARNING WARNING WARNING

JUMBLE®

Unscramble these four Jumbles, one letter to each square, to form four ordinary words.

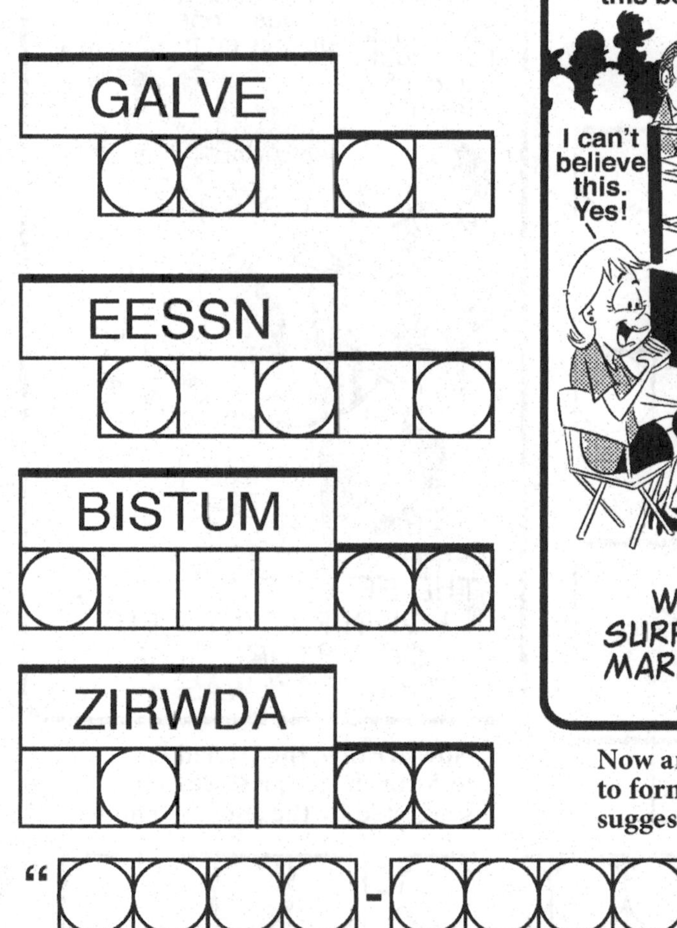
GALVE
EESSN
BISTUM
ZIRWDA

We have a great view of this beautiful moment.
I can't believe this. Yes!
You've knocked me out!
WHEN THE BOXER SURPRISED HER WITH A MARRIAGE PROPOSAL, SHE HAD A ---

Now arrange the circled letters to form the surprise answer, as suggested by the above cartoon.

Print answer here

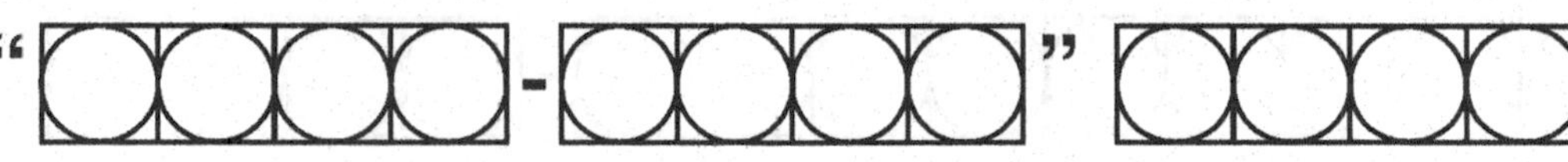

PUZZLE 98

WARNING WARNING WARNING WARNING WARNING WARNING WARNING

JUMBLE®

Unscramble these four Jumbles, one letter to each square, to form four ordinary words.

INBOS
OLCLE
GRYEES
DARELY
This looks like it took a lot of thought.
It started as part of an ensemble, but I think it stands alone. It should be viewed from below.
THE EFFORT AUGUSTE RODIN PUT INTO HIS SCULPTURE "THE THINKER," WAS ---

Now arrange the circled letters to form the surprise answer, as suggested by the above cartoon.

Print answer here “◯◯◯◯◯◯◯◯-◯◯◯◯”

PUZZLE 99

Unscramble these four Jumbles, one letter to each square, to form four ordinary words.

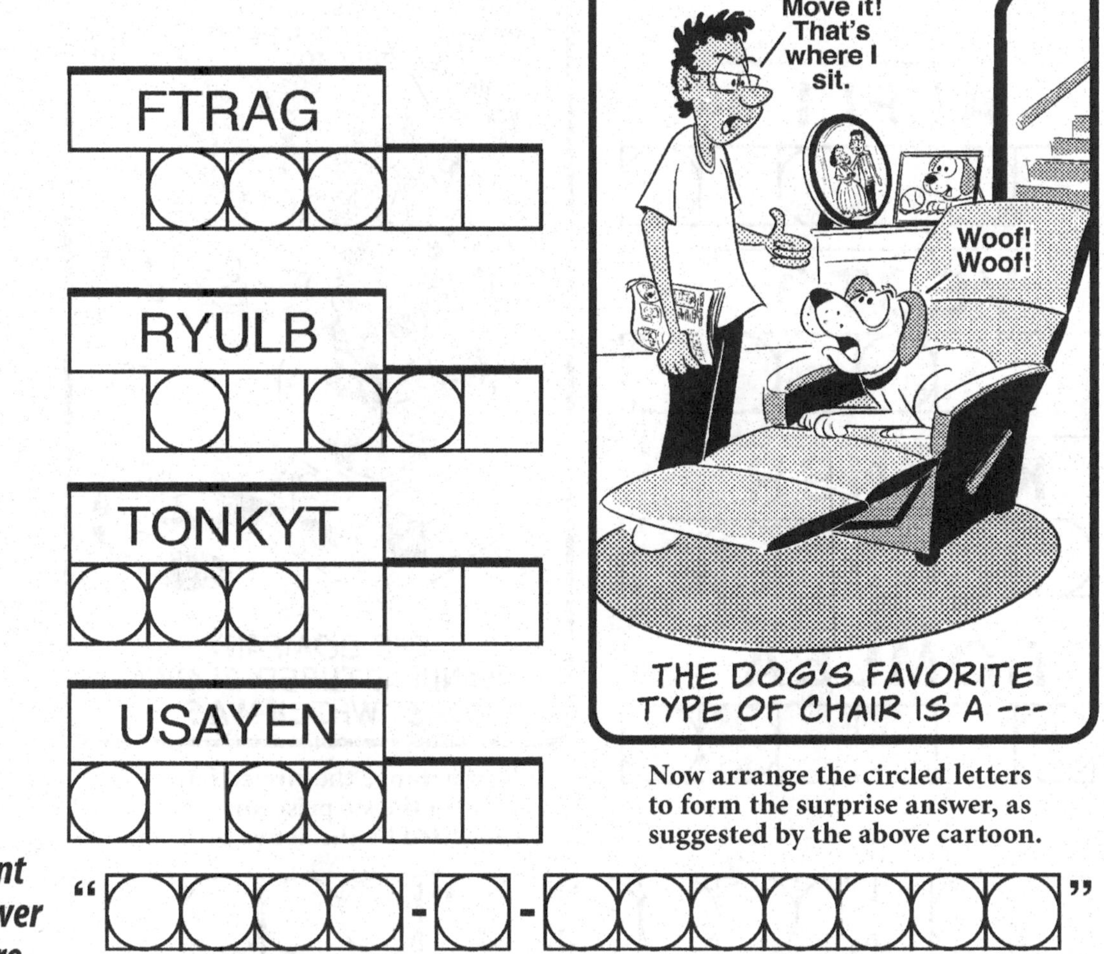
FTRAG
RYULB
TONKYT
USAYEN
Hey! Move it! That's where I sit.
Woof! Woof!
THE DOG'S FAVORITE TYPE OF CHAIR IS A ---

Now arrange the circled letters to form the surprise answer, as suggested by the above cartoon.

Print answer here "____-_-________"

PUZZLE 100

WARNING WARNING WARNING WARNING WARNING WARNING WARNING

JUMBLE®

Unscramble these four Jumbles, one letter to each square, to form four ordinary words.

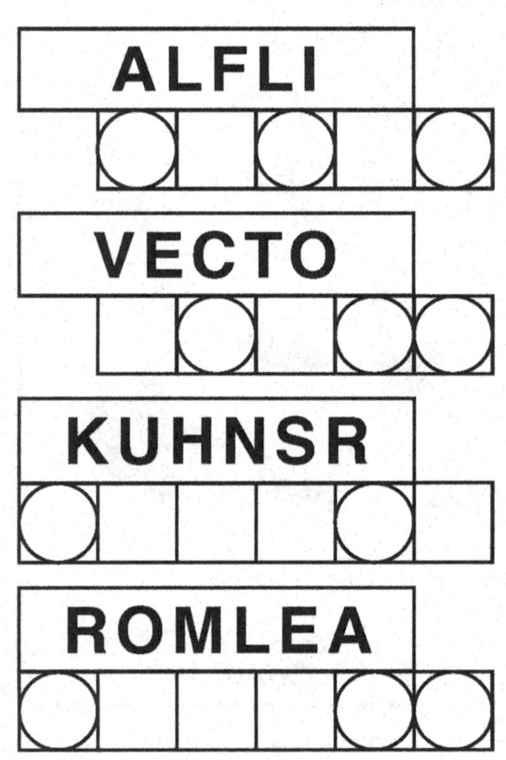

ALFLI
VECTO
KUHNSR
ROMLEA

It was difficult, but we found the finest clown cobblers. We're the biggest in the industry.
These size 24s fit great.
THE COMPANY MANUFACTURED CLOWN SHOES, WHICH WAS ---

Now arrange the circled letters to form the surprise answer, as suggested by the above cartoon.

Print answer here

“”

PUZZLE 101

WARNING WARNING WARNING WARNING WARNING WARNING WARNING

JUMBLE®

Unscramble these four Jumbles, one letter to each square, to form four ordinary words.

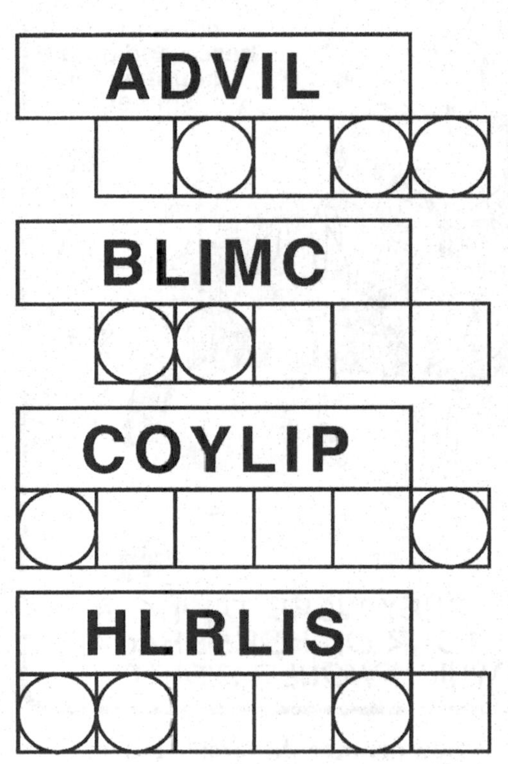

ADVIL
BLIMC
COYLIP
HLRLIS

I can fly!
We need to try scene one. Get down! Is anybody listening?
Can I be Peter Pan instead?
I'm stuck!
DIRECTING THE THIRD-GRADERS' STAGE PERFORMANCE WAS TOUGH AND CERTAINLY NOT ---

Now arrange the circled letters to form the surprise answer, as suggested by the above cartoon.

Print answer here

PUZZLE 102

WARNING WARNING WARNING WARNING WARNING WARNING WARNING

JUMBLE®

Unscramble these four Jumbles, one letter to each square, to form four ordinary words.

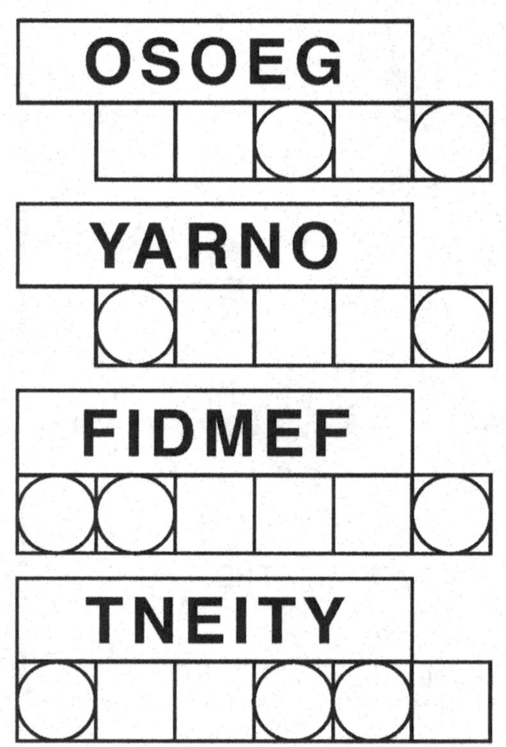
OSOEG
YARNO
FIDMEF
TNEITY

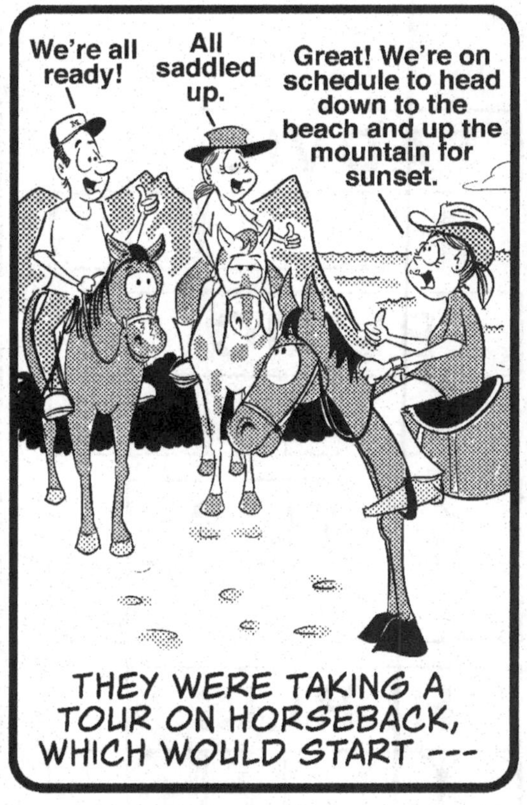
We're all ready!
All saddled up.
Great! We're on schedule to head down to the beach and up the mountain for sunset.
THEY WERE TAKING A TOUR ON HORSEBACK, WHICH WOULD START ---

Now arrange the circled letters to form the surprise answer, as suggested by the above cartoon.

Print answer here ""  

WARNING WARNING WARNING WARNING WARNING WARNING WARNING

JUMBLE®

Unscramble these four Jumbles, one letter to each square, to form four ordinary words.

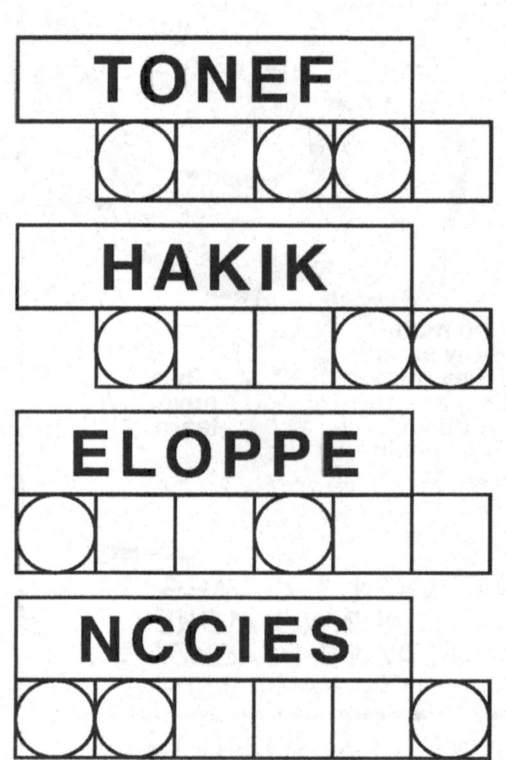
TONEF
HAKIK
ELOPPE
NCCIES

He didn't see it coming.
Three ball in the side, eight ball in the corner.
FOR THE POOL SHARK, IT WAS LIKE STEALING MONEY, THANKS TO HIS ABILITY TO ---

Now arrange the circled letters to form the surprise answer, as suggested by the above cartoon.

Print answer here

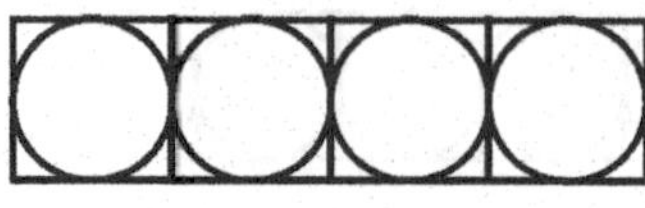

PUZZLE 104

JUMBLE®

Unscramble these four Jumbles, one letter to each square, to form four ordinary words.

MRUST
SLUPH
PUABET
ECINET

My system isn't working.
21! Dealer wins.
No matter how smart they think they are, the odds are always in our favor.
They never learn.
WHEN IT COMES TO WINNING MONEY PLAYING BLACKJACK, IT'S HARD TO ---

Now arrange the circled letters to form the surprise answer, as suggested by the above cartoon.

Print answer here

PUZZLE 105

WARNING WARNING WARNING WARNING WARNING WARNING WARNING

JUMBLE®

Unscramble these four Jumbles, one letter to each square, to form four ordinary words.

SHYUK
LORDE
UBPHAC
PLATEL

Sweet Tooth Bistro
Oh! That sounds good.
Please, come in!
Oh! Look at that.
SHE OPENED HER STORE IN A BUSY NEIGHBORHOOD. NOW SHE NEEDED CUSTOMERS TO ---

Now arrange the circled letters to form the surprise answer, as suggested by the above cartoon.

Print answer here  "  "

WARNING WARNING WARNING WARNING WARNING WARNING WARNING

JUMBLE®

Unscramble these four Jumbles, one letter to each square, to form four ordinary words.

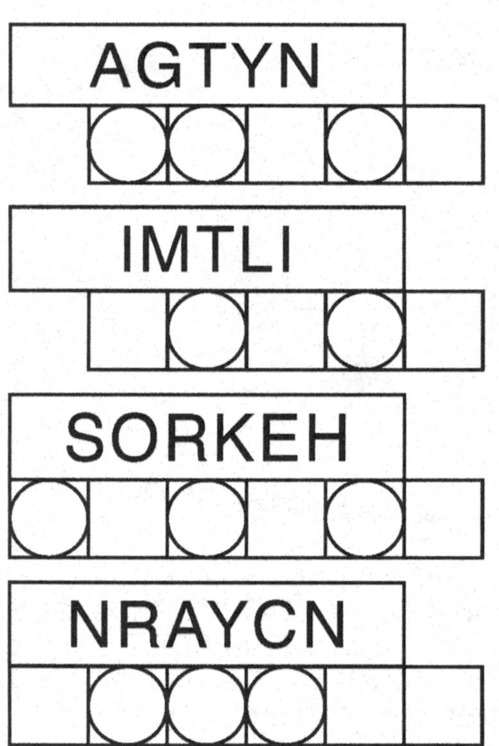
AGTYN
IMTLI
SORKEH
NRAYCN

The cameras will help me keep an eye out on league night.
I hope we finally catch him.
THEY'D HAD SOME THEFTS AT THE BOWLING ALLEY AND WORRIED THE THIEF MIGHT ---

Now arrange the circled letters to form the surprise answer, as suggested by the above cartoon.

Print answer here

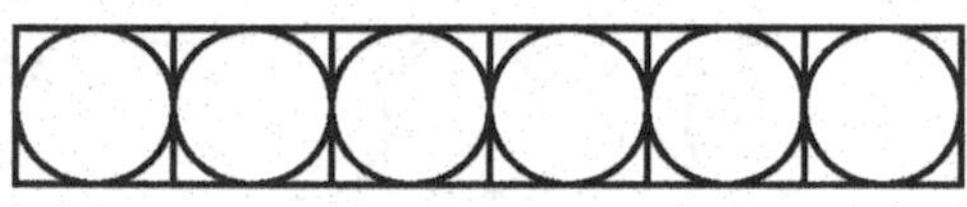

PUZZLE 107

WARNING WARNING WARNING WARNING WARNING WARNING WARNING

JUMBLE®

Unscramble these four Jumbles, one letter to each square, to form four ordinary words.

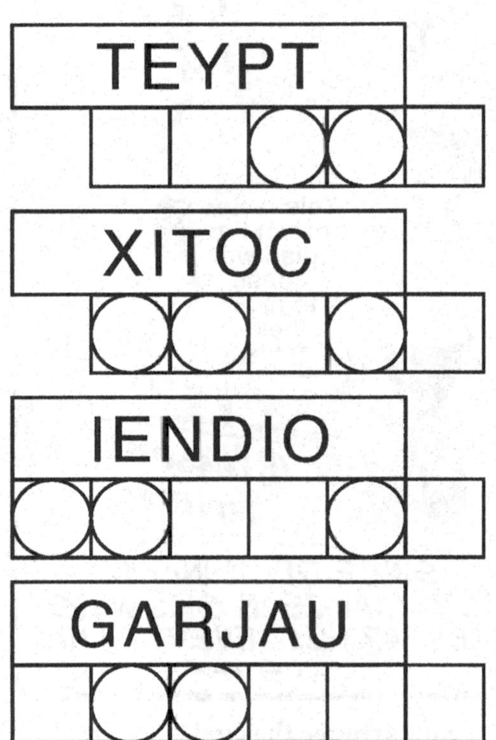
TEYPT
XITOC
IENDIO
GARJAU

C'mon! Don't be a chicken! Go for it!
Hey!
WHEN BILLY DARED HIS BUDDY TO JUMP THE FENCE, HE WAS TRYING TO ---

Now arrange the circled letters to form the surprise answer, as suggested by the above cartoon.

Print answer here "" HIM  

PUZZLE 108

WARNING WARNING WARNING WARNING WARNING WARNING WARNING

JUMBLE®

Unscramble these four Jumbles, one letter to each square, to form four ordinary words.

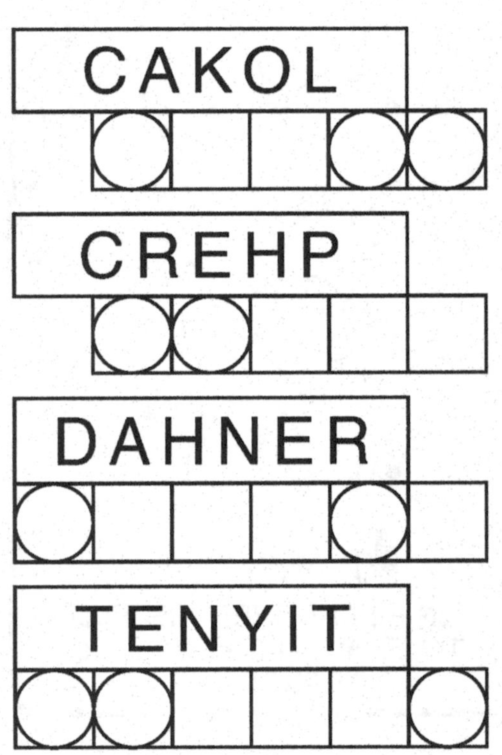
CAKOL
CREHP
DAHNER
TENYIT

This tastes great! I'm glad we chose to grow these.
Me too! It's all been good.
Blossom Farms
SINCE DECIDING TO SPECIALIZE IN GROWING NECTARINES, EVERYTHING WAS ---

Now arrange the circled letters to form the surprise answer, as suggested by the above cartoon.

Print answer here

PUZZLE 109

WARNING WARNING WARNING WARNING WARNING WARNING WARNING

JUMBLE®

Unscramble these four Jumbles, one letter to each square, to form four ordinary words.

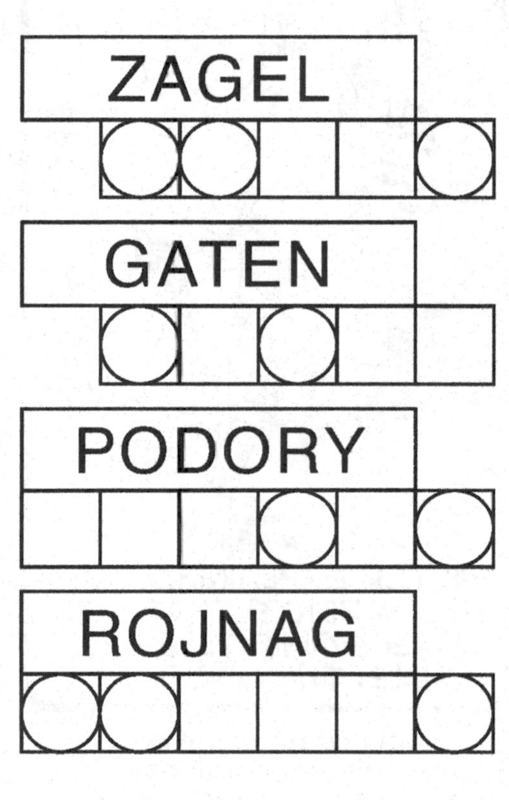

ZAGEL
GATEN
PODORY
ROJNAG

Look! They used to have buttons instead of a zipper.
Look at these bell bottoms!
THE DISPLAY AT THE LEVI STRAUSS MUSEUM SHOWED THE DUNGAREES' ---

Now arrange the circled letters to form the surprise answer, as suggested by the above cartoon.

Print answer here 

WARNING WARNING WARNING WARNING WARNING WARNING WARNING

JUMBLE®

Unscramble these four Jumbles, one letter to each square, to form four ordinary words.

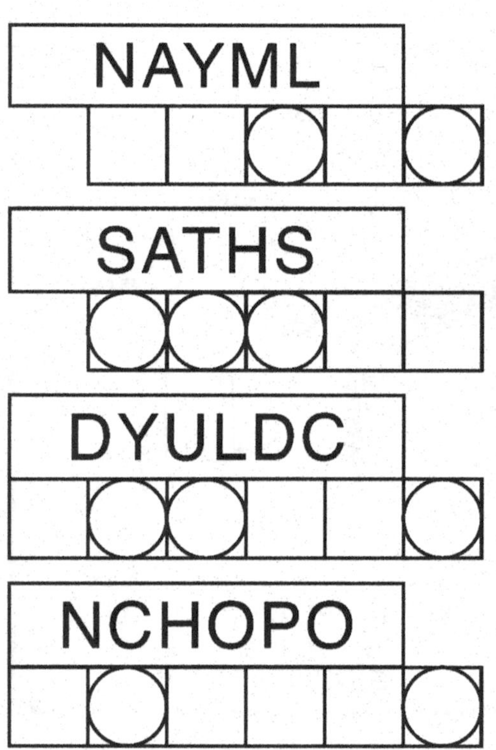
NAYML
SATHS
DYULDC
NCHOPO

What's that, dear? Why aren't you talking?
Not the mime thing, again!
AFTER EXPLAINING TO HIS PARENTS THAT HE WAS GOING TO BE A MIME, THEY SAID ---

Now arrange the circled letters to form the surprise answer, as suggested by the above cartoon.

Print answer here

PUZZLE 111

WARNING WARNING WARNING WARNING WARNING WARNING WARNING

JUMBLE®

Unscramble these four Jumbles, one letter to each square, to form four ordinary words.

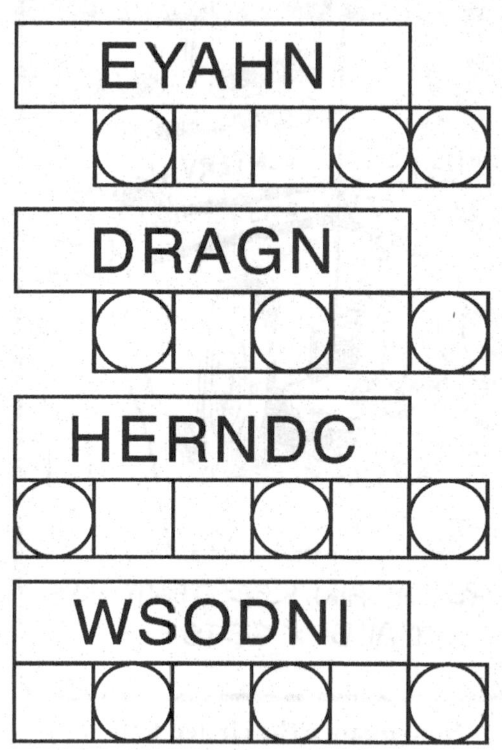

EYAHN
DRAGN
HERNDC
WSODNI

I'd fold if I were you.
You're bluffing.
I think I'm good. All in!
BEING DEALT A ROYAL FLUSH AND WINNING ---

Now arrange the circled letters to form the surprise answer, as suggested by the above cartoon.

Print answer here

PUZZLE 112

WARNING WARNING WARNING WARNING WARNING WARNING WARNING

JUMBLE®

Unscramble these four Jumbles, one letter to each square, to form four ordinary words.

RVPIE

CABIS

CEDDEA

RUYTEK

Today's Guest JUMBLERS are
TOM BATIUK & DAN DAVIS
creators of CRANKSHAFT
CENTERVIL
0013
11-12
YET AGAIN, KEESTERMAN'S MAILBOX GETS ---

Now arrange the circled letters to form the surprise answer, as suggested by the above cartoon.

Print answer here 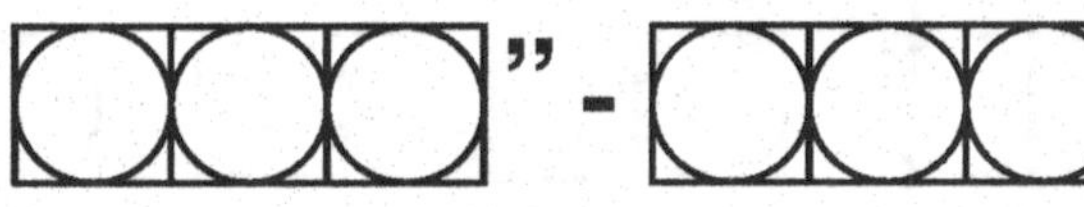

PUZZLE 113

WARNING WARNING WARNING WARNING WARNING WARNING WARNING

JUMBLE®

Unscramble these four Jumbles, one letter to each square, to form four ordinary words.

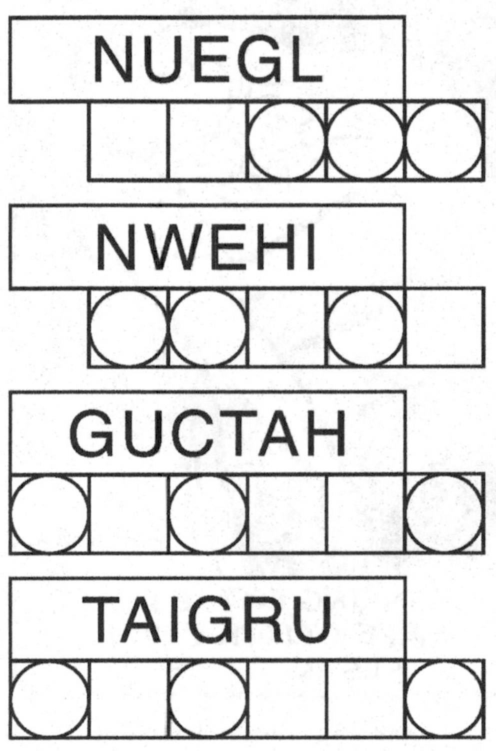

NUEGL
NWEHI
GUCTAH
TAIGRU

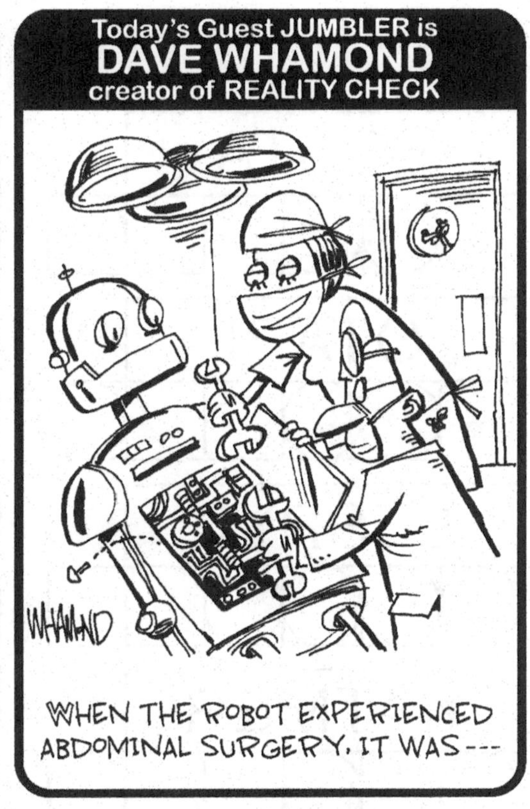

Today's Guest JUMBLER is
DAVE WHAMOND
creator of REALITY CHECK
WHAMOND
WHEN THE ROBOT EXPERIENCED ABDOMINAL SURGERY, IT WAS---

Now arrange the circled letters to form the surprise answer, as suggested by the above cartoon.

Print answer here

PUZZLE 114

WARNING WARNING WARNING WARNING WARNING WARNING WARNING

JUMBLE®

Unscramble these four Jumbles, one letter to each square, to form four ordinary words.

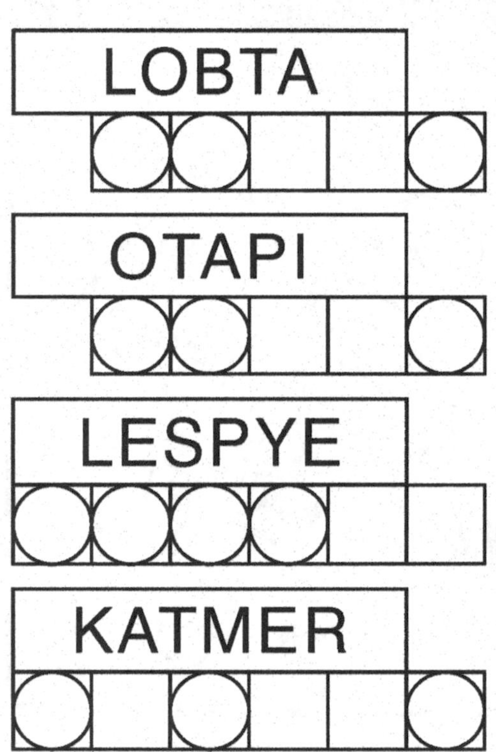

LOBTA
OTAPI
LESPYE
KATMER

Today's Guest JUMBLER is
SANDRA BELL-LUNDY
creator of BETWEEN FRIENDS
Bell-Lundy
DRINKING COFFEE AFTER THREE O'CLOCK CAUSED SUSAN A ---

Now arrange the circled letters to form the surprise answer, as suggested by the above cartoon.

Print answer here

PUZZLE 115

WARNING WARNING WARNING WARNING WARNING WARNING WARNING

JUMBLE®

Unscramble these four Jumbles, one letter to each square, to form four ordinary words.

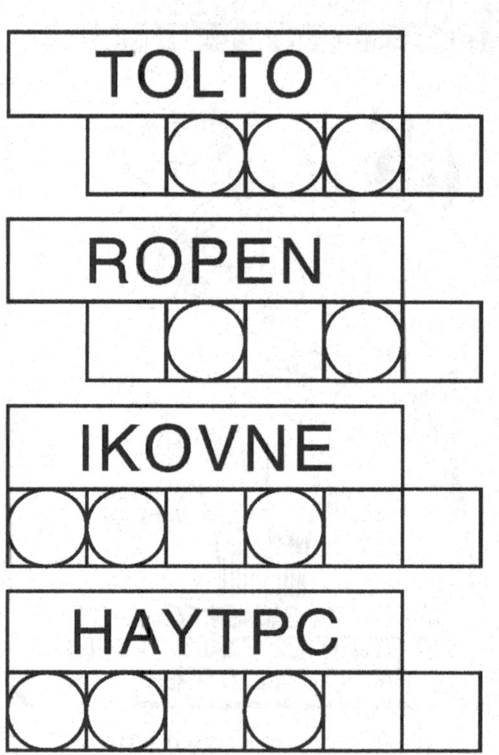

TOLTO
ROPEN
IKOVNE
HAYTPC

Today's Guest JUMBLER is
ED STECKLEY
MAD MAGAZINE & RUBE GOLDBERG
Illustrator
A
B
C
D
E
F
G
H
I
J
K
WHEN YOUNG RUBE GOLDBERG WANTED TO CATCH A MOUSE, HE BUILT A ---

Now arrange the circled letters to form the surprise answer, as suggested by the above cartoon.

Print answer here

PUZZLE 116

WARNING WARNING WARNING WARNING WARNING WARNING WARNING

JUMBLE®

Unscramble these four Jumbles, one letter to each square, to form four ordinary words.

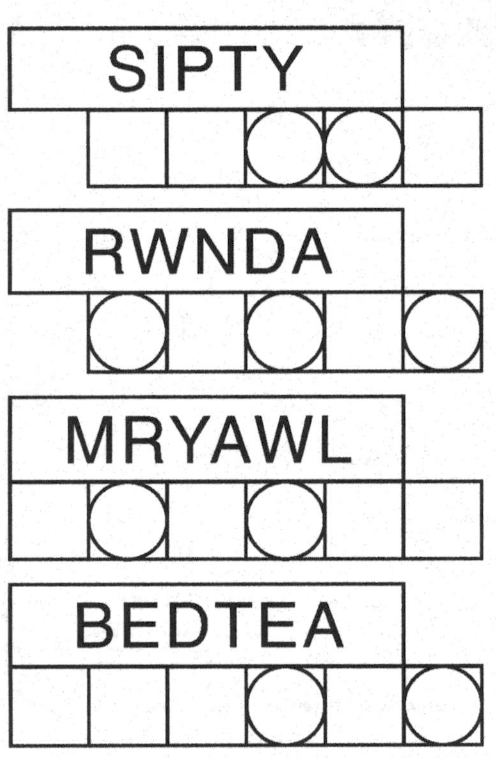

SIPTY
RWNDA
MRYAWL
BEDTEA

Today's Guest JUMBLERS are
HECTOR CANTÚ &
CARLOS CASTELLANOS
creators of BALDO

AFTER TÍA CARMEN FORGOT TO STUFF HER BAKED TREATS, BALDO CALLED THEM ---

Now arrange the circled letters to form the surprise answer, as suggested by the above cartoon.

Print answer here

PUZZLE 117

WARNING WARNING WARNING WARNING WARNING WARNING WARNING

JUMBLE®

Unscramble these four Jumbles, one letter to each square, to form four ordinary words.

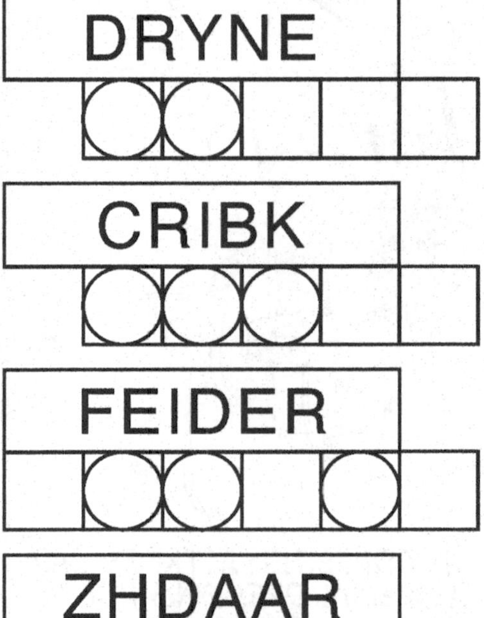
DRYNE
CRIBK
FEIDER
ZHDAAR

Today's Guest JUMBLER is
CHAD CARPENTER
creator of TUNDRA
OW.
ONE OF THE DRAWBACKS OF A POLAR BEAR'S DIET

Now arrange the circled letters to form the surprise answer, as suggested by the above cartoon.

Print answer here

PUZZLE 118

WARNING WARNING WARNING WARNING WARNING WARNING WARNING

JUMBLE®

Unscramble these four Jumbles, one letter to each square, to form four ordinary words.

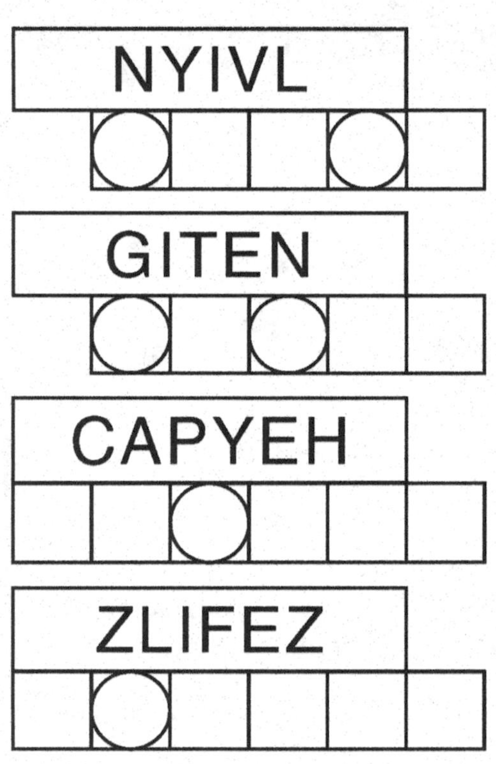
NYIVL
GITEN
CAPYEH
ZLIFEZ

Wow! This is all for you?
I had this built so I could see myself from every angle.
THE CONCEITED ACTRESS HAD A SPECIAL DRESSING ROOM AND WAS SHOWING OFF HER ---

Now arrange the circled letters to form the surprise answer, as suggested by the above cartoon.

Print answer here

PUZZLE 119

WARNING WARNING WARNING WARNING WARNING WARNING WARNING

Unscramble these four Jumbles, one letter to each square, to form four ordinary words.

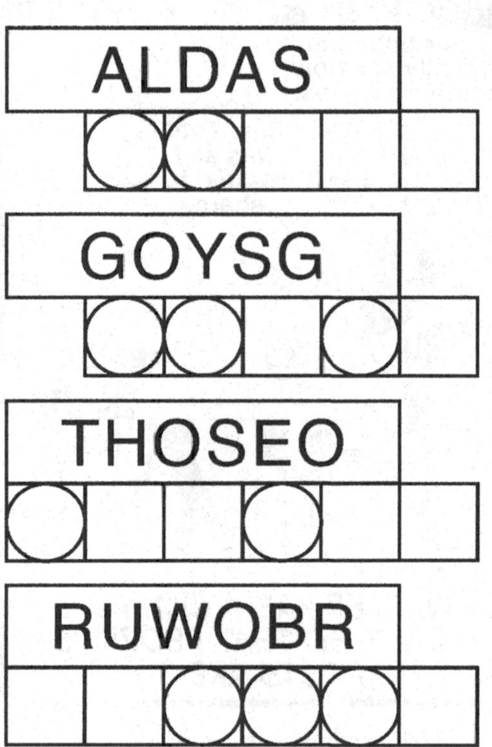
ALDAS
GOYSG
THOSEO
RUWOBR

Just ask your neighbors how much they love their new lawn.
That's what they said. I've seen your work. I like it.
THE SOD COMPANY'S APPROACH TO GETTING NEW BUSINESS WAS ---

Now arrange the circled letters to form the surprise answer, as suggested by the above cartoon.

Print answer here

PUZZLE
120

WARNING WARNING WARNING WARNING WARNING WARNING WARNING

JUMBLE®

Unscramble these four Jumbles, one letter to each square, to form four ordinary words.

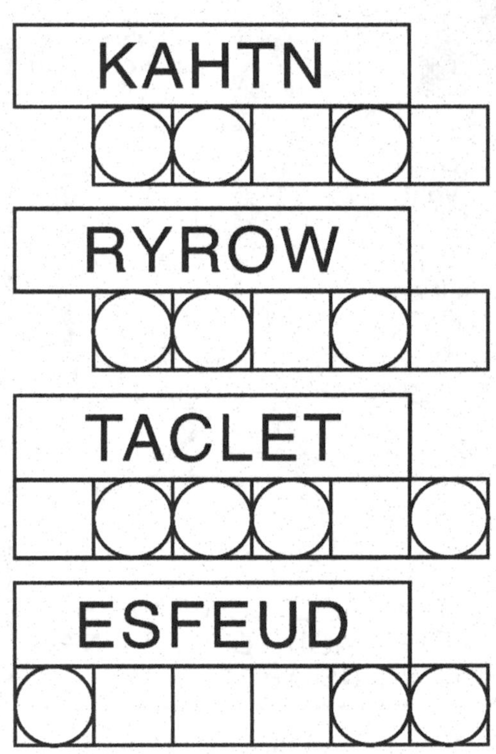
KAHTN
RYROW
TACLET
ESFEUD

Your post didn't really say how the party was.
It was fine. That was all I wanted to share.
TWITTER HAS A CHARACTER LIMIT SO THAT PEOPLE'S POSTS ARE ---

Now arrange the circled letters to form the surprise answer, as suggested by the above cartoon.

Print answer here

WARNING WARNING WARNING WARNING WARNING WARNING WARNING

JUMBLE®

Unscramble these four Jumbles, one letter to each square, to form four ordinary words.

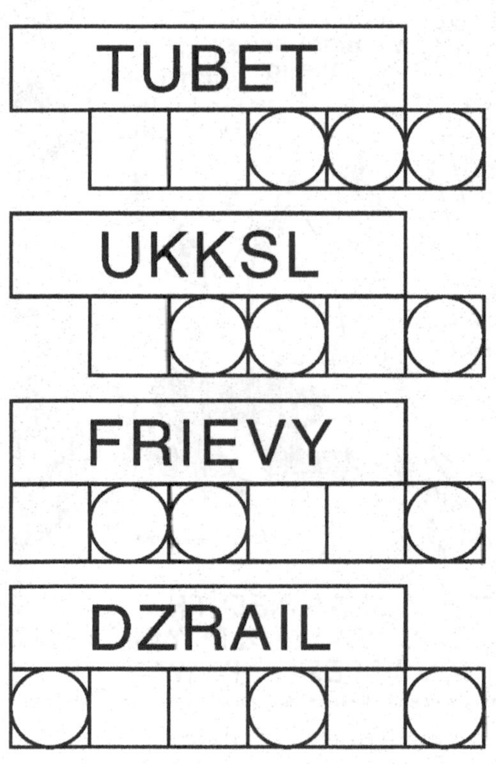
TUBET
UKKSL
FRIEVY
DZRAIL

Now, we need to baste the bird every 30 minutes.
No, we don't. I don't baste anymore. It's been brined.
KISS the COOK
THE THANKSGIVING COOKS' CONVERSATION BECAME SERIOUS WHEN THEY ---

Now arrange the circled letters to form the surprise answer, as suggested by the above cartoon.

Print answer here

JUMBLE®

Unscramble these four Jumbles, one letter to each square, to form four ordinary words.

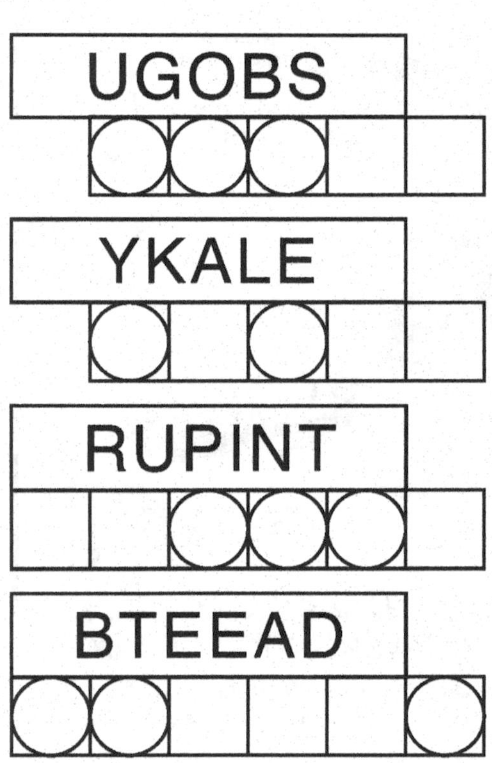
UGOBS
YKALE
RUPINT
BTEEAD

We need to shore that up or we might have a cave-in.
There's a lot here to mine.
THEY EXAMINED THE WALL IN THE NEW GOLD MINE AND DISCOVERED IT WAS ---

Now arrange the circled letters to form the surprise answer, as suggested by the above cartoon.

Print answer here "" - 

PUZZLE 123

WARNING WARNING WARNING WARNING WARNING WARNING WARNING

JUMBLE®

Unscramble these four Jumbles, one letter to each square, to form four ordinary words.

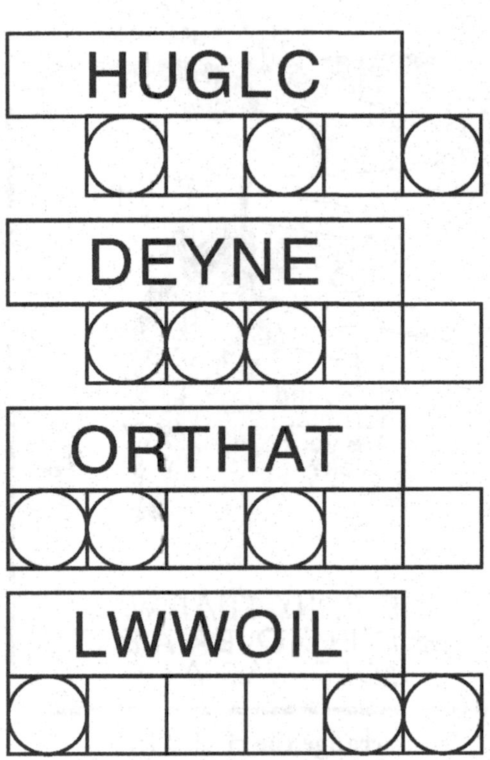
HUGLC
DEYNE
ORTHAT
LWWOIL

BIG PIG ROAST
We've pulled out all the stops.
This is going to be quite the feast.
THEY WANTED IT TO BE THE BEST PIG ROAST EVER, SO THEY ---

Now arrange the circled letters to form the surprise answer, as suggested by the above cartoon.

Print answer here

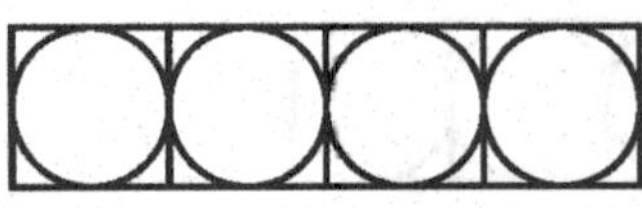

PUZZLE 124

WARNING WARNING WARNING WARNING WARNING WARNING WARNING

JUMBLE®

Unscramble these four Jumbles, one letter to each square, to form four ordinary words.

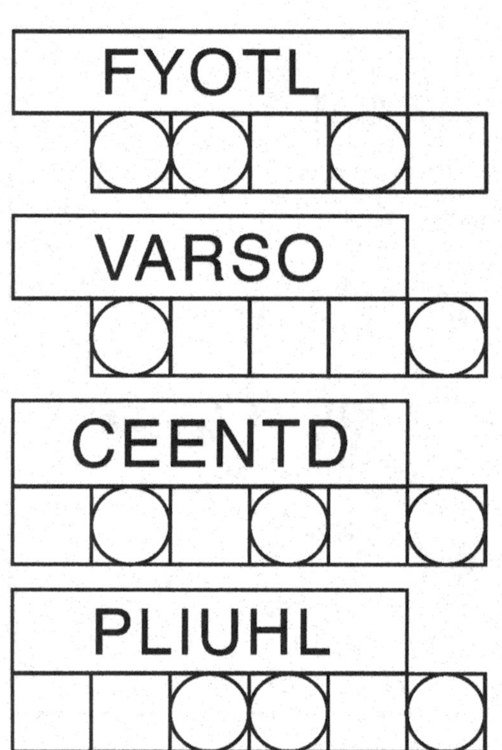

FYOTL
VARSO
CEENTD
PLIUHL

Trig! You need to go back to the barn and get some rest.
I'm getting better.
You sound horrible. Are you sick?
THE PONY THAT WAS GETTING OVER A BAD COLD WAS A ---

Now arrange the circled letters to form the surprise answer, as suggested by the above cartoon.

Print answer here

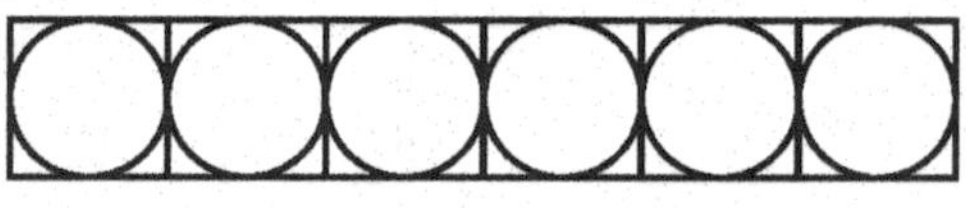

PUZZLE
125

WARNING WARNING WARNING WARNING WARNING WARNING WARNING

JUMBLE®

Unscramble these four Jumbles, one letter to each square, to form four ordinary words.

FCOSF
OILGO
DIDFEE
LOBBBE

Now, give me this scene as an everyday conversation.
Do you have a job for me, Sal?
Do you want to deliver for me?
THE MOVIE SET IN THE PIZZA PARLOR SHOWED A ---

Now arrange the circled letters to form the surprise answer, as suggested by the above cartoon.

Print answer here

WARNING WARNING WARNING WARNING WARNING WARNING WARNING

JUMBLE®

Unscramble these four Jumbles, one letter to each square, to form four ordinary words.

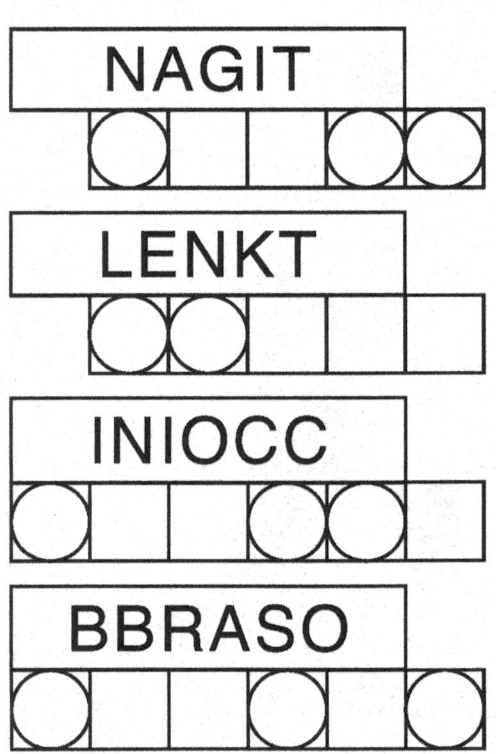
NAGIT
LENKT
INIOCC
BBRASO

Excuse me, ma'am! Would you be interested in a free checking account?
No fees? That sounds good.
We really need to get people inside.
FREE CHECKING TODAY!
FINANCIAL INSTITUTIONS NEED YOUR BUSINESS AND ARE ---

Now arrange the circled letters to form the surprise answer, as suggested by the above cartoon.

Print answer here

PUZZLE 127

WARNING WARNING WARNING WARNING WARNING WARNING WARNING

JUMBLE®

Unscramble these four Jumbles, one letter to each square, to form four ordinary words.

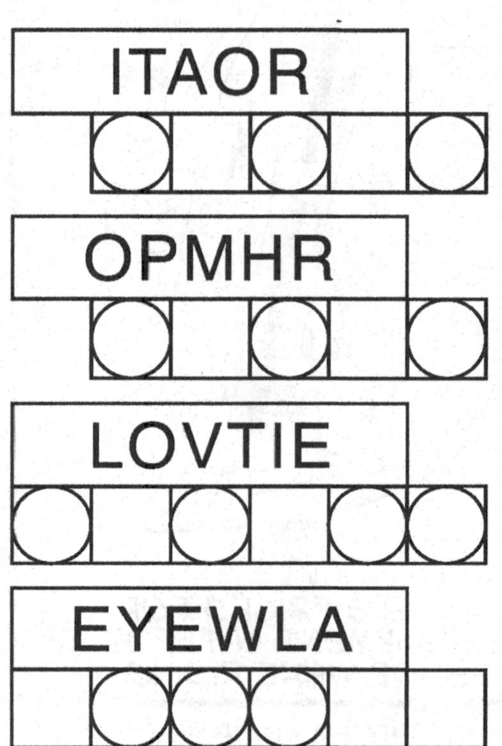
ITAOR
OPMHR
LOVTIE
EYEWLA

We'll be able to see all of Paris from up there.
At 1,063 feet, it will be the world's tallest structure.
You are amazing, Gustave!
GUSTAVE EIFFEL WAS SHORTER THAN MOST PARISIANS, BUT HE WAS ABLE TO ---

Now arrange the circled letters to form the surprise answer, as suggested by the above cartoon.

Print answer here

PUZZLE 128

WARNING WARNING WARNING WARNING WARNING WARNING WARNING

JUMBLE®

Unscramble these four Jumbles, one letter to each square, to form four ordinary words.

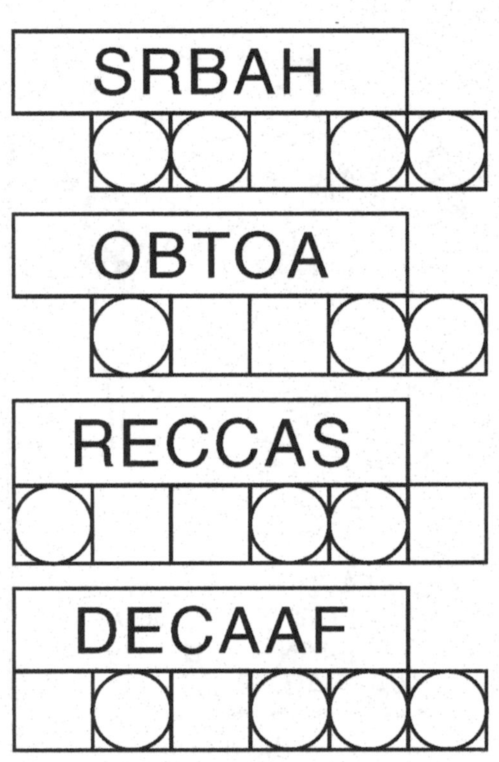

SRBAH
OBTOA
RECCAS
DECAAF

Are these all more expensive than last week?
Yep. We had to add 20% to everything.
$400
$600
$550
THE PRICES FOR EQUIPMENT IN THE SURF SHOP WERE RISING ---

Now arrange the circled letters to form the surprise answer, as suggested by the above cartoon.

Print answer here

PUZZLE
129

WARNING WARNING WARNING WARNING WARNING WARNING WARNING

JUMBLE®

Unscramble these four Jumbles, one letter to each square, to form four ordinary words.

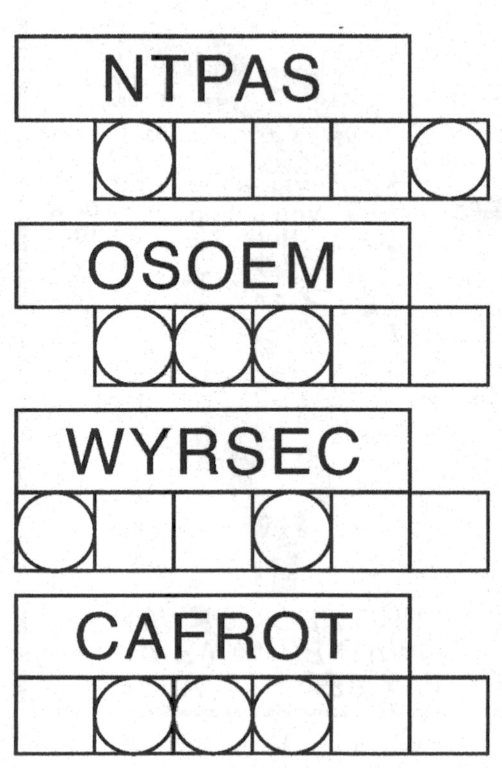
NTPAS
OSOEM
WYRSEC
CAFROT

One day, I'm going to be a pro quarterback!
Congratulations! Your dreams came true!
Where did you find that?
JUMBLERS
HIS PREDICTION THAT HE'D BECOME A QUARTERBACK IN THE NFL HAD ---

Now arrange the circled letters to form the surprise answer, as suggested by the above cartoon.

Print answer here

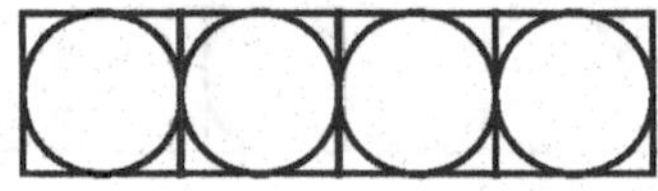  

JUMBLE®

Unscramble these four Jumbles, one letter to each square, to form four ordinary words.

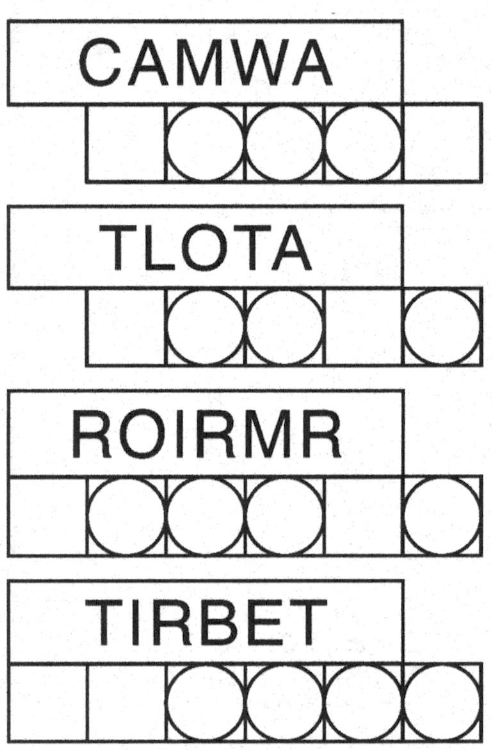
CAMWA
TLOTA
ROIRMR
TIRBET

Where are you taking Betsy?
I'm hauling her to the shop. She broke down again.
THE TRUCK DRIVER WHO BECAME A FARMER HAD A ---

Now arrange the circled letters to form the surprise answer, as suggested by the above cartoon.

Print answer here

PUZZLE 131

WARNING WARNING WARNING WARNING WARNING WARNING WARNING

Unscramble these four Jumbles, one letter to each square, to form four ordinary words.

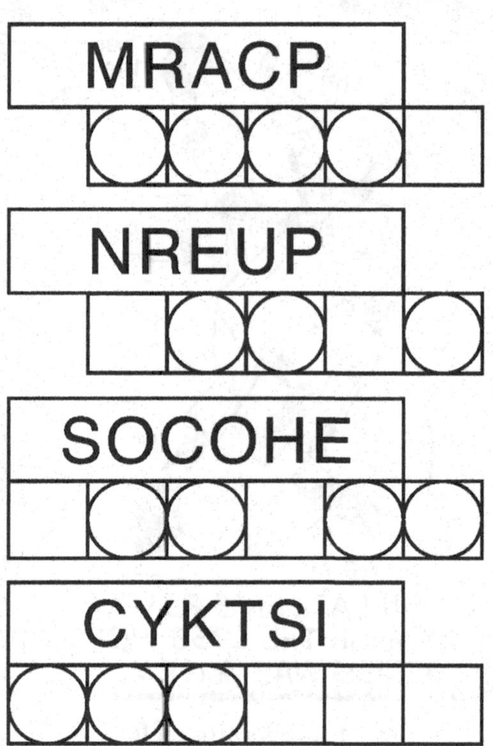

MRACP
NREUP
SOCOHE
CYKTSI

They were just marked half off. You'll love them!
That sounds great!
SECOND SPIN
$300
$200
WHEN SHE FOUND OUT THE HEADPHONES WERE ON SALE, IT WAS ---

Now arrange the circled letters to form the surprise answer, as suggested by the above cartoon.

Print answer here

PUZZLE 132

WARNING WARNING WARNING WARNING WARNING WARNING WARNING

JUMBLE®

Unscramble these four Jumbles, one letter to each square, to form four ordinary words.

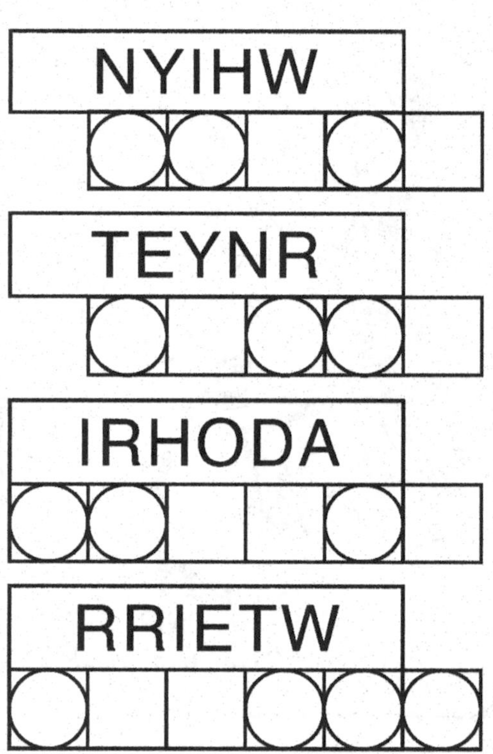

NYIHW
TEYNR
IRHODA
RRIETW

I've never seen so many strikes go over the plate!
Thanks for the great target, Yogi!
DON LARSEN'S PERFECT GAME IN THE 1956 WORLD SERIES WAS A GEM, ---

Now arrange the circled letters to form the surprise answer, as suggested by the above cartoon.

Print answer here

WARNING WARNING WARNING WARNING WARNING WARNING WARNING

JUMBLE®

Unscramble these four Jumbles, one letter to each square, to form four ordinary words.

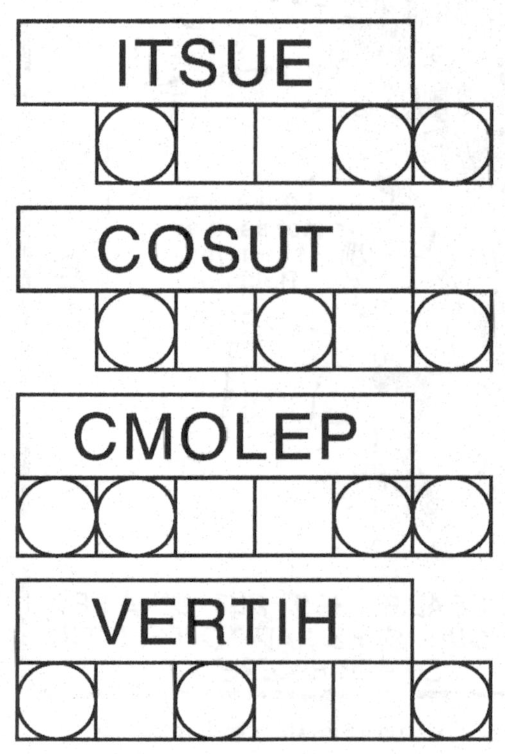
ITSUE
COSUT
CMOLEP
VERTIH

Put me down for another par.
What? You put two in the pond. You had a triple bogey at best!
HE'D CAUGHT HIS OPPONENT CHEATING, AND NOW THE GOLFER HAD A ---

Now arrange the circled letters to form the surprise answer, as suggested by the above cartoon.

Print answer here

WARNING WARNING WARNING WARNING WARNING WARNING WARNING

PUZZLE 134

JUMBLE®

Unscramble these four Jumbles, one letter to each square, to form four ordinary words.

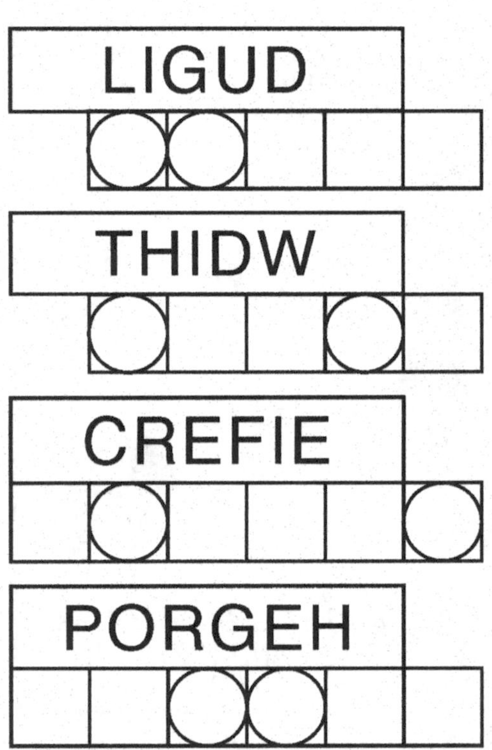
LIGUD
THIDW
CREFIE
PORGEH

We'll stay here for you.
I guess I'm not as fit as I thought. Hold on!

BECAUSE HE'D PUT ON A FEW POUNDS, HE HAD TO TELL THE OTHER HIKERS TO---

Now arrange the circled letters to form the surprise answer, as suggested by the above cartoon.

Print answer here " ◯◯◯◯◯◯ " ◯◯

PUZZLE 135

WARNING WARNING WARNING WARNING WARNING WARNING WARNING

Unscramble these four Jumbles, one letter to each square, to form four ordinary words.

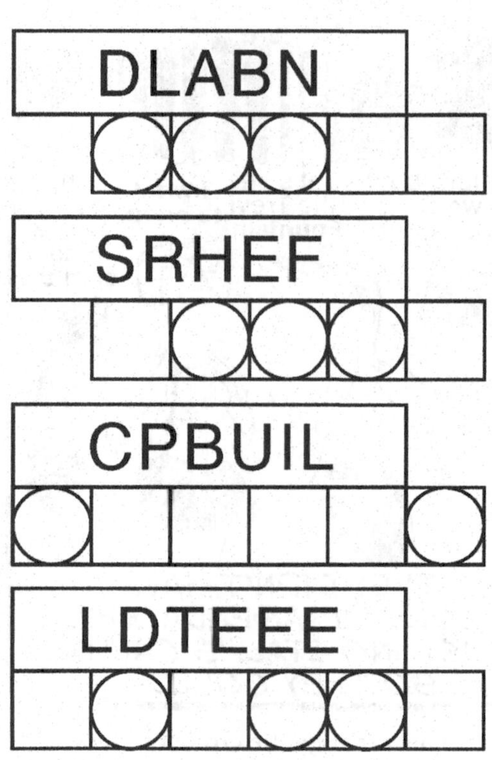

DLABN
SRHEF
CPBUIL
LDTEEE

It's nice that so many people are here honoring Memorial Day.
WYANDOTTE, MICHIGAN
AMERICAN LEGION
POST 217
THE CROWD OF PEOPLE ATTENDING THE MEMORIAL DAY PARADE WAS ---

Now arrange the circled letters to form the surprise answer, as suggested by the above cartoon.

Print answer here

JUMBLE®

Unscramble these four Jumbles, one letter to each square, to form four ordinary words.

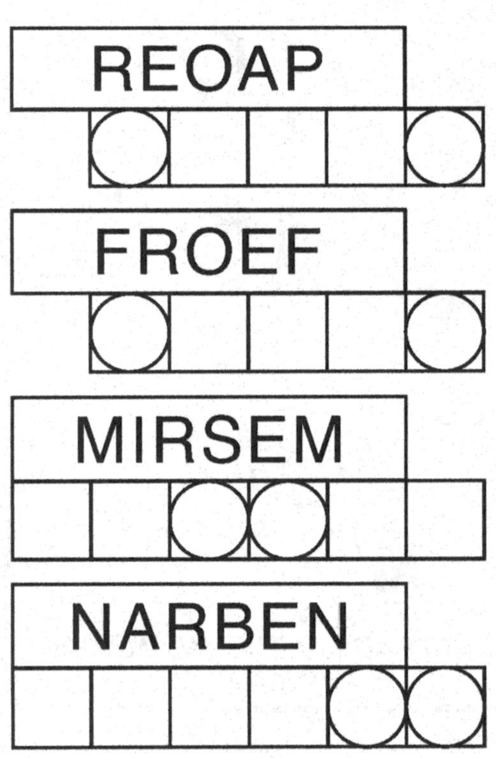
REOAP
FROEF
MIRSEM
NARBEN

How 'bout we go to the Forum?
Let's see the Trevi Fountain.
I want to shop.
I'm going to the cata-combs.
THEY DIDN'T HAVE A SPECIFIC AGENDA WHILE VISITING ITALY'S CAPITAL, SO THEY COULD ---

Now arrange the circled letters to form the surprise answer, as suggested by the above cartoon.

Print answer here

PUZZLE 137

WARNING WARNING WARNING WARNING WARNING WARNING WARNING

JUMBLE®

Unscramble these four Jumbles, one letter to each square, to form four ordinary words.

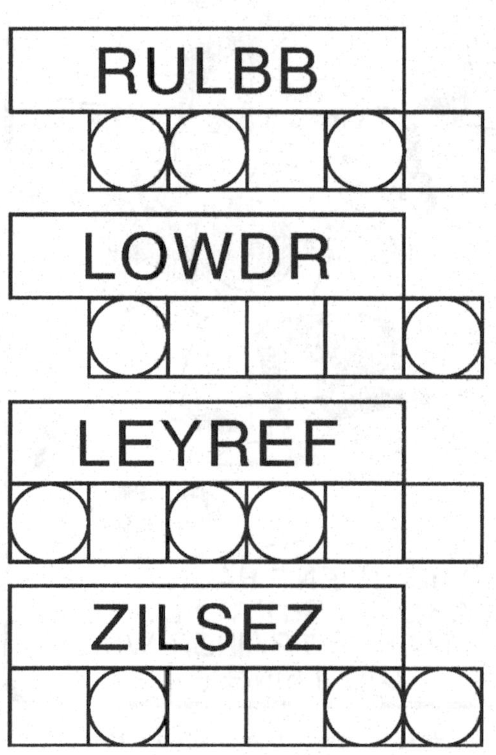
RULBB
LOWDR
LEYREF
ZILSEZ

What's the deal with these?
We are promoting these as active underwear. They're made from high-tech material.
BEFORE STARTING THE NEW AD CAMPAIGN, THE UNDERWEAR MODEL WAS ---

Now arrange the circled letters to form the surprise answer, as suggested by the above cartoon.

Print answer here

WARNING WARNING WARNING WARNING WARNING WARNING WARNING

PUZZLE 138

JUMBLE®

Unscramble these four Jumbles, one letter to each square, to form four ordinary words.

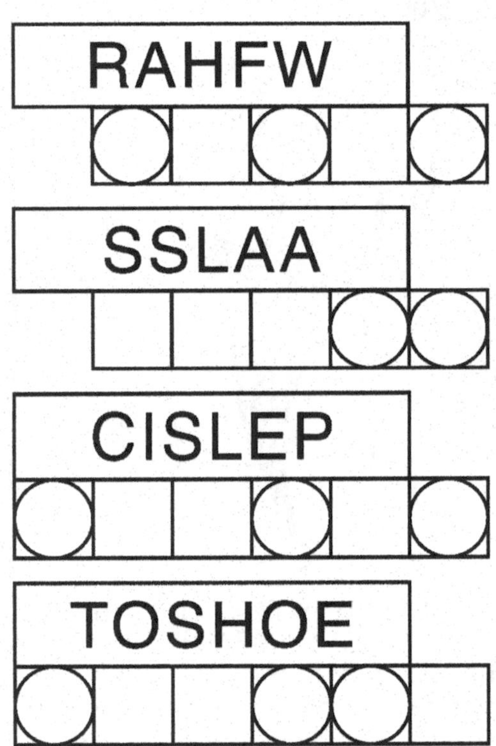

RAHFW
SSLAA
CISLEP
TOSHOE

You got this! If you listen to me, I will get you in shape!
Yes, ma'am.

THE CLIENT HAD LITTLE CHOICE BUT TO LISTEN TO HER TRAINER WHO DID THINGS ---

Now arrange the circled letters to form the surprise answer, as suggested by the above cartoon.

Print answer here

PUZZLE
139

WARNING WARNING WARNING WARNING WARNING WARNING WARNING

JUMBLE®

Unscramble these four Jumbles, one letter to each square, to form four ordinary words.

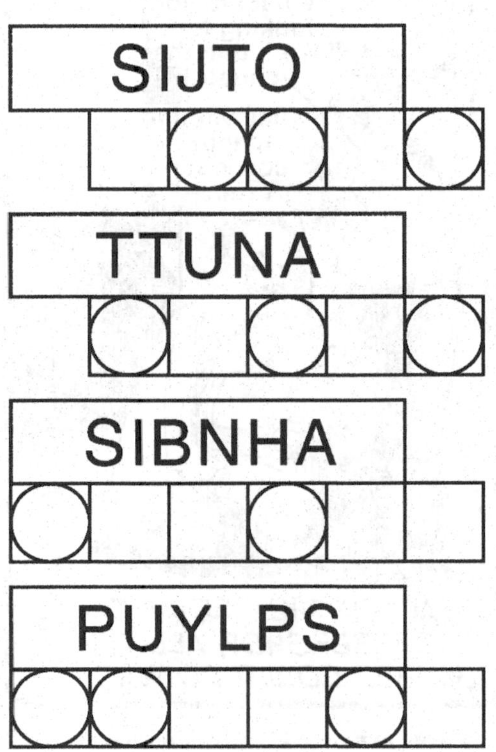

SIJTO
TTUNA
SIBNHA
PUYLPS

DANDY MAN
It's looking sharp.
We followed all your designs.
THE NEW TUXEDO RENTAL STORE WAS DESIGNED BY ITS OWNER AND ---

Now arrange the circled letters to form the surprise answer, as suggested by the above cartoon.

Print answer here

PUZZLE 140

WARNING WARNING WARNING WARNING WARNING WARNING WARNING

JUMBLE®

Unscramble these four Jumbles, one letter to each square, to form four ordinary words.

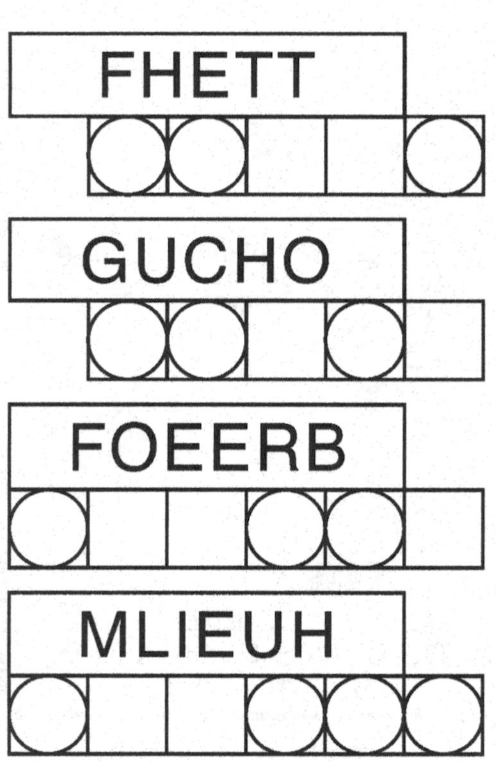

FHETT
GUCHO
FOEERB
MLIEUH

What are you looking for? We found the cause.
My vintage magazine collection is ruined.
AFTER THE FIRE AT THE BARBERSHOP, ALL THE BARBER COULD DO WAS ---

Now arrange the circled letters to form the surprise answer, as suggested by the above cartoon.

Print answer here

PUZZLE 141

WARNING WARNING WARNING WARNING WARNING WARNING WARNING

JUMBLE®

Unscramble these four Jumbles, one letter to each square, to form four ordinary words.

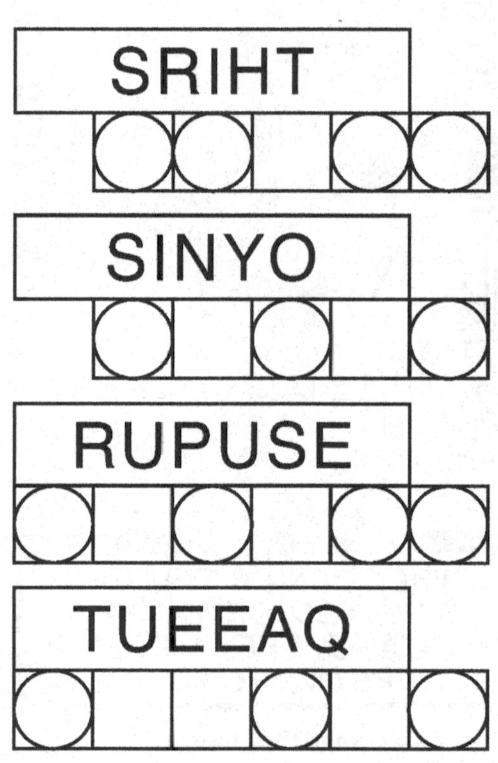
SRIHT
SINYO
RUPUSE
TUEEAQ

I can't believe you're 70! Way to go!
I may be slowing down, but I'll be up here on my next birthday too!
THE HIKER WHO ALWAYS CLIMBED TO THE SUMMIT ON HER BIRTHDAY WAS GETTING ---

Now arrange the circled letters to form the surprise answer, as suggested by the above cartoon.

Print answer here

PUZZLE 142

WARNING WARNING WARNING WARNING WARNING WARNING WARNING

JUMBLE®

Unscramble these four Jumbles, one letter to each square, to form four ordinary words.

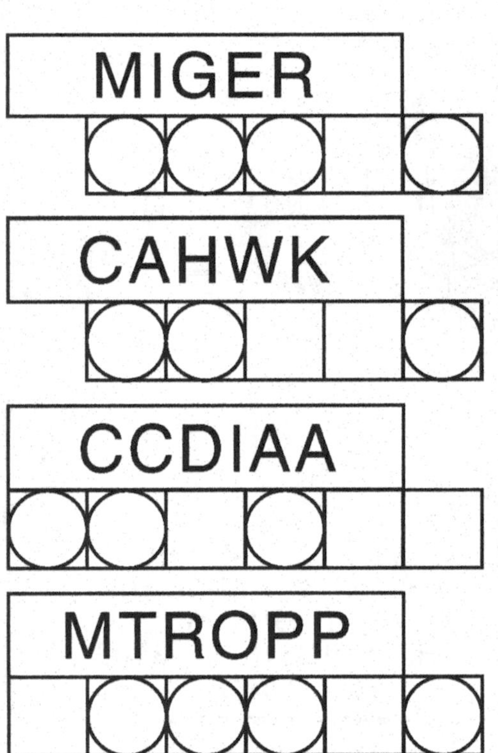

MIGER
CAHWK
CCDIAA
MTROPP

Good evening! We'd like to start off with a card trick.
This is a great trick.
WHEN PENN & TELLER STEPPED ONTO THE STAGE, THEY WERE READY TO ---

Now arrange the circled letters to form the surprise answer, as suggested by the above cartoon.

Print answer here

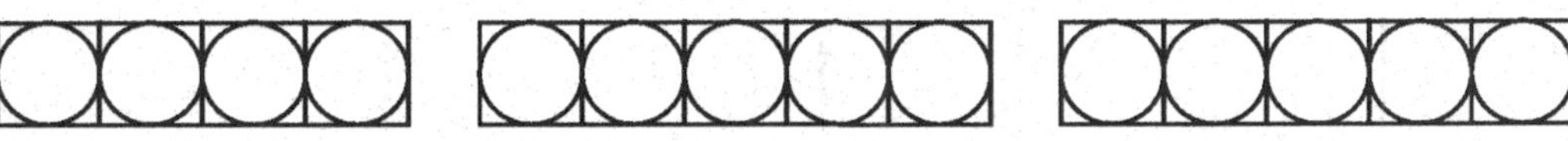

PUZZLE 143

WARNING WARNING WARNING WARNING WARNING WARNING WARNING

Unscramble these four Jumbles, one letter to each square, to form four ordinary words.

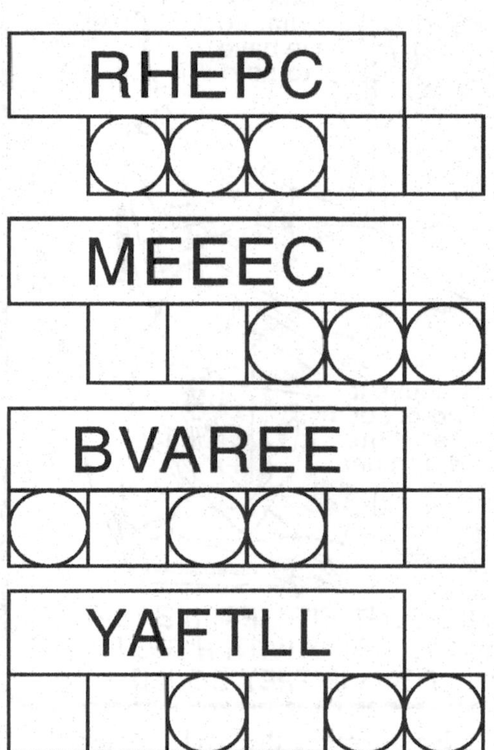
RHEPC
MEEEC
BVAREE
YAFTLL

This fits you perfectly, Owlman.
This makes my outfit. Thanks!
She's the best!
THE TAILOR SPECIALIZED IN SUPERHERO COSTUMES AND WAS ---

Now arrange the circled letters to form the surprise answer, as suggested by the above cartoon.

Print answer here

JUMBLE®

Unscramble these four Jumbles, one letter to each square, to form four ordinary words.

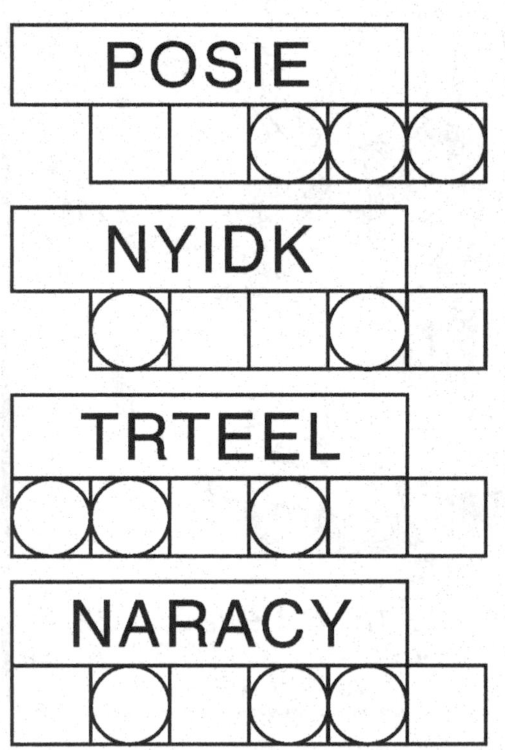
POSIE
NYIDK
TRTEEL
NARACY

We love you, Champ. What do we have to do?
Show us the money!
I love it here. Let's split the difference.
THE BEST PITCHER IN BASEBALL WOULD STAY WITH HIS CURRENT TEAM IF THEY COULD ---

Now arrange the circled letters to form the surprise answer, as suggested by the above cartoon.

Print answer here

PUZZLE
145

WARNING WARNING WARNING WARNING WARNING WARNING WARNING

JUMBLE®

Unscramble these four Jumbles, one letter to each square, to form four ordinary words.

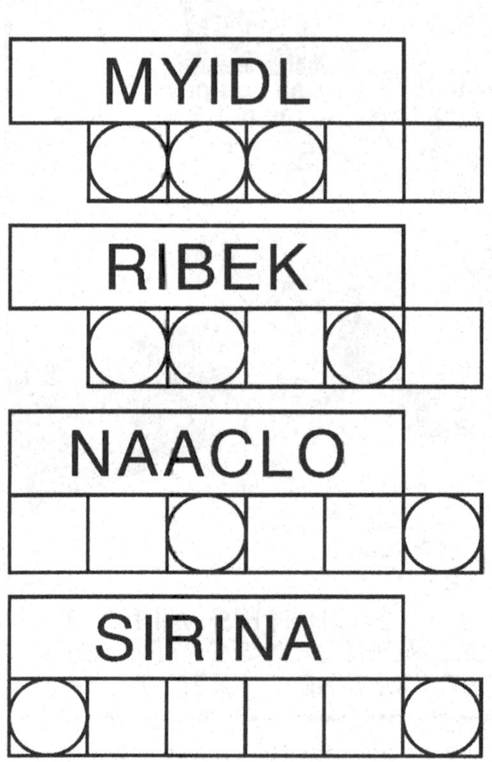

MYIDL
RIBEK
NAACLO
SIRINA

We're going to need to be careful.
I won't forget.
WARNING
GRIZZLY ACTIVITY IS HIGH
HIKE AT YOUR OWN RISK

THEY SAW THE WARNING ABOUT THE GRIZZLIES WHICH THEY WOULD NEED TO ---

Now arrange the circled letters to form the surprise answer, as suggested by the above cartoon.

Print answer here

PUZZLE 146

WARNING WARNING WARNING WARNING WARNING WARNING WARNING

JUMBLE®

Unscramble these four Jumbles, one letter to each square, to form four ordinary words.

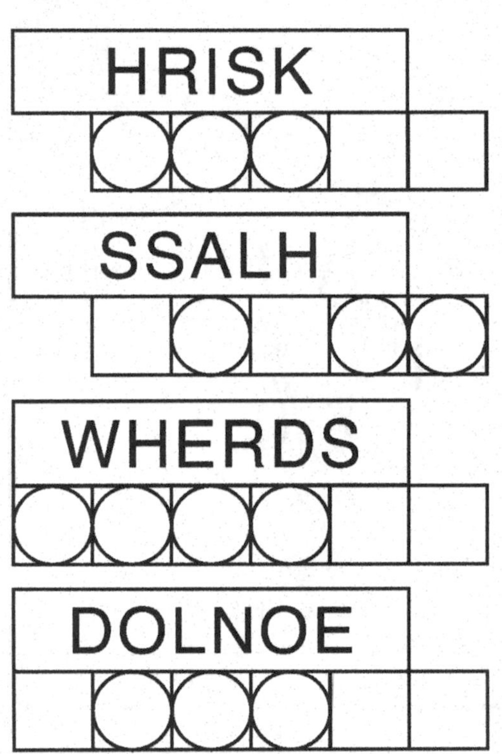

HRISK
SSALH
WHERDS
DOLNOE

1st 6
2nd 3
3rd 1
UNOFFICIAL
One minute. The results aren't official yet.
Whoa! Way to go, Max!
Can you pay me now?
CASHIER
TO CASH IN HIS WINNING BELMONT STAKES "TRIFECTA" TICKET, HE'D NEED TO ---

Now arrange the circled letters to form the surprise answer, as suggested by the above cartoon.

Print answer here

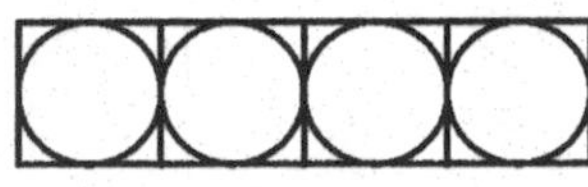

PUZZLE 147

WARNING WARNING WARNING WARNING WARNING WARNING WARNING

JUMBLE®

Unscramble these four Jumbles, one letter to each square, to form four ordinary words.

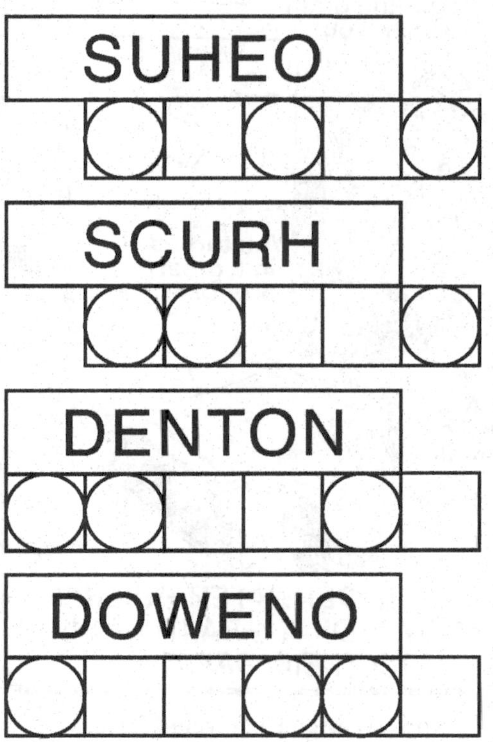

SUHEO
SCURH
DENTON
DOWENO

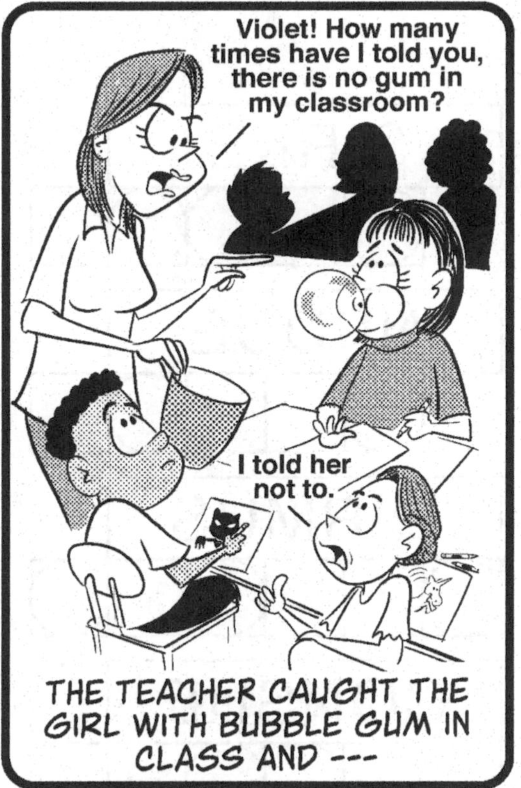

Violet! How many times have I told you, there is no gum in my classroom?
I told her not to.
THE TEACHER CAUGHT THE GIRL WITH BUBBLE GUM IN CLASS AND ---

Now arrange the circled letters to form the surprise answer, as suggested by the above cartoon.

Print answer here

WARNING WARNING WARNING WARNING WARNING WARNING WARNING

JUMBLE®

Unscramble these four Jumbles, one letter to each square, to form four ordinary words.

SIRKB

NPDUE

QIRMUS

CONSHE

What?
We got the grant!
Thank you!
You turned in a great proposal.
Now we can really go deep!
THE UNDERWATER SCIENCE TEAM WON A GRANT THANKS TO THEIR GREAT ---

Now arrange the circled letters to form the surprise answer, as suggested by the above cartoon.

Print answer here “□□□-□□□□□□□”

PUZZLE 149

WARNING WARNING WARNING WARNING WARNING WARNING WARNING

JUMBLE®

Unscramble these four Jumbles, one letter to each square, to form four ordinary words.

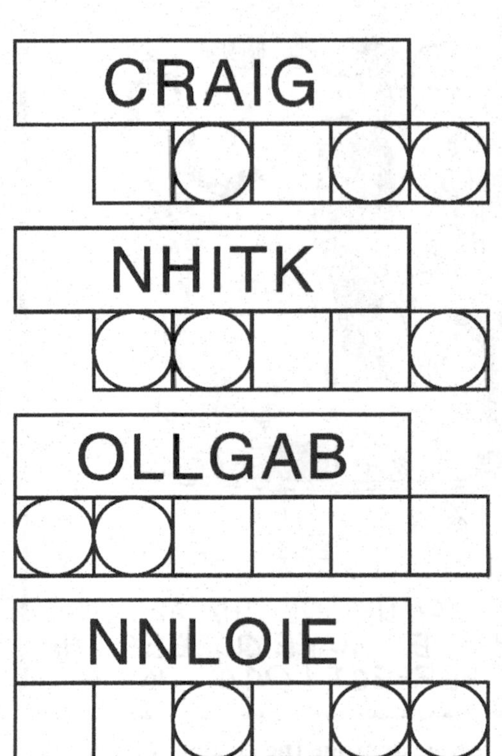
CRAIG
NHITK
OLLGAB
NNLOIE

I know it's late, but we have a lot more to cover.
May I use the water closet?
KING ARTHUR'S MEETING AT THE ROUND TABLE WAS TURNING INTO AN ---

Now arrange the circled letters to form the surprise answer, as suggested by the above cartoon.

Print answer here

WARNING WARNING WARNING WARNING WARNING WARNING WARNING

JUMBLE®

Unscramble these four Jumbles, one letter to each square, to form four ordinary words.

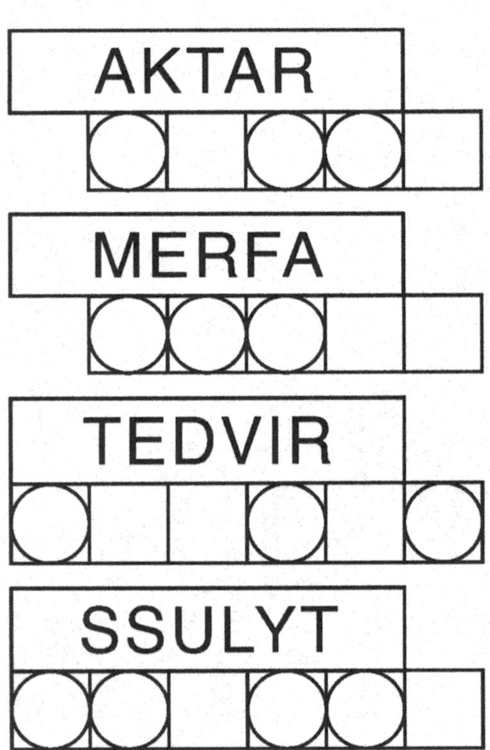
AKTAR
MERFA
TEDVIR
SSULYT

Welcome! Take your pelts inside; we'll negotiate a deal.
SAMUEL DE CHAMPLAIN HELPED MAKE QUEBEC THE PERFECT LOCATION ---

Now arrange the circled letters to form the surprise answer, as suggested by the above cartoon.

Print answer here “”  

PUZZLE 151

WARNING WARNING WARNING WARNING WARNING WARNING WARNING

Unscramble these four Jumbles, one letter to each square, to form four ordinary words.

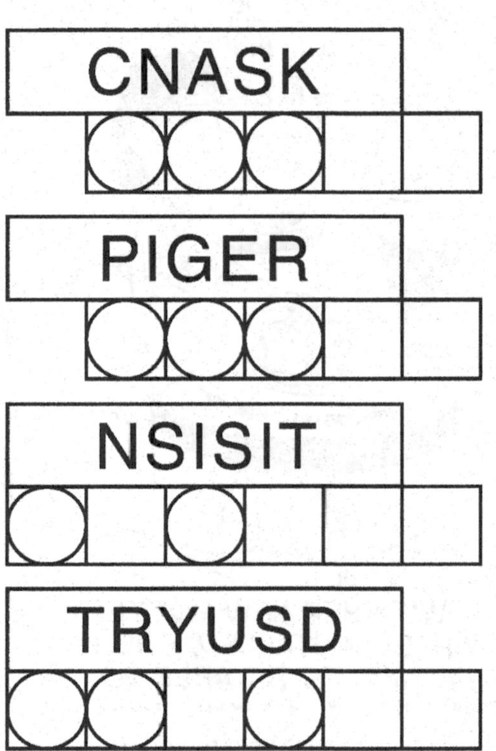

CNASK
PIGER
NSISIT
TRYUSD

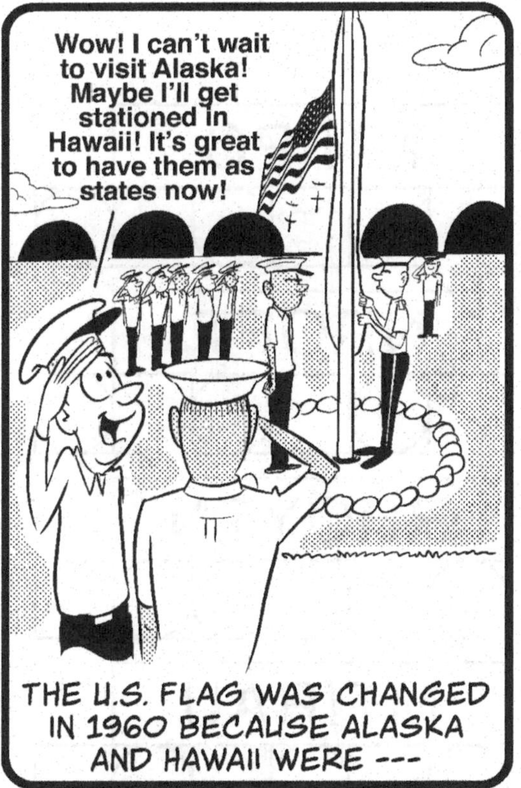

Wow! I can't wait to visit Alaska! Maybe I'll get stationed in Hawaii! It's great to have them as states now!
THE U.S. FLAG WAS CHANGED IN 1960 BECAUSE ALASKA AND HAWAII WERE ---

Now arrange the circled letters to form the surprise answer, as suggested by the above cartoon.

Print answer here

PUZZLE 152

WARNING WARNING WARNING WARNING WARNING WARNING WARNING

JUMBLE®

Unscramble these four Jumbles, one letter to each square, to form four ordinary words.

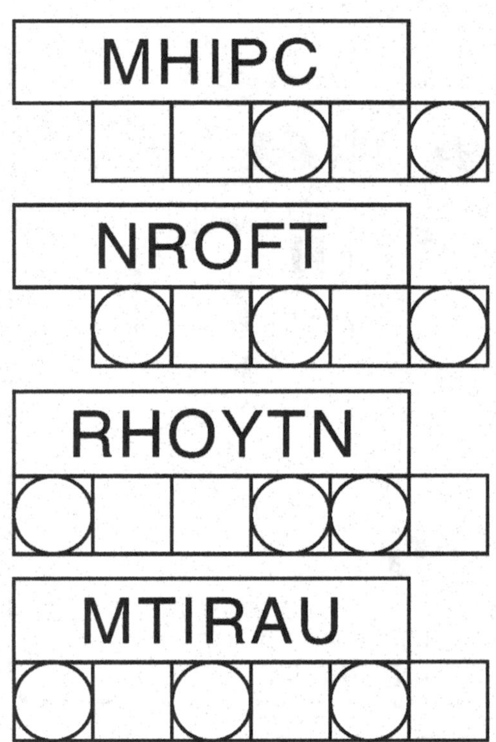

MHIPC
NROFT
RHOYTN
MTIRAU

Wow! You are just cranking these out with the new wheel!
It's great! It will certainly help me "urn" a living.
WITH HER NEW POTTERY WHEEL INSTALLED, SHE WAS HOPING TO BE ABLE TO ---

Now arrange the circled letters to form the surprise answer, as suggested by the above cartoon.

Print answer here

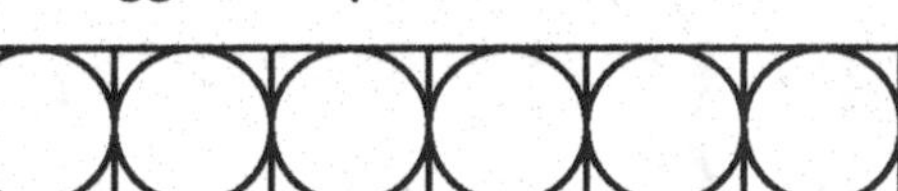

WARNING WARNING WARNING WARNING WARNING WARNING WARNING

PUZZLE 153

JUMBLE®

Unscramble these four Jumbles, one letter to each square, to form four ordinary words.

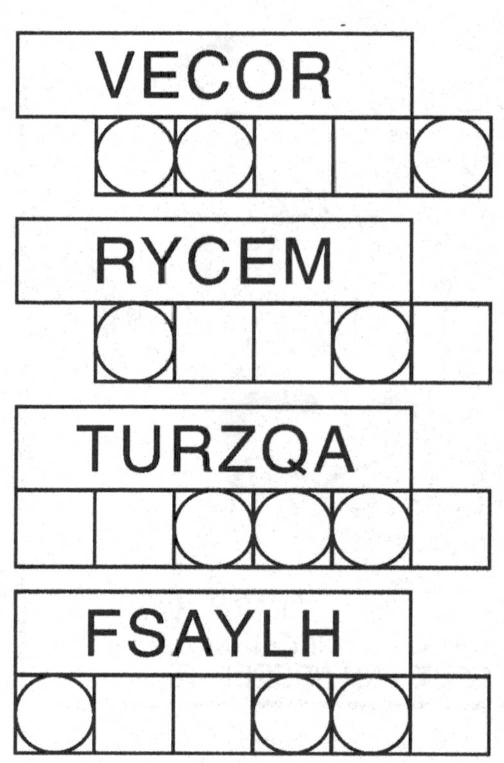

VECOR
RYCEM
TURZQA
FSAYLH

I dislike itching so much, I decided to work on a repellent solution.
You certainly are thorough.
TO FILE FOR HIS MOSQUITO REPELLENT PATENT IN 1946, SAMUEL GERTLER STARTED ---

Now arrange the circled letters to form the surprise answer, as suggested by the above cartoon.

Print answer here

PUZZLE 154

WARNING WARNING WARNING WARNING WARNING WARNING WARNING

JUMBLE®

Unscramble these four Jumbles, one letter to each square, to form four ordinary words.

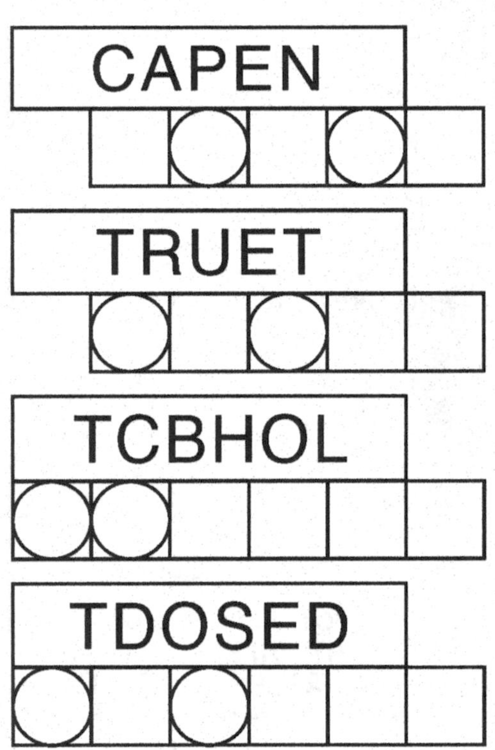

CAPEN
TRUET
TCBHOL
TDOSED

I'm not sure I can afford to make it to another harvest.
Don't worry. I'm going to float you the cash.
THE HAY FARM WAS STRUGGLING DUE TO HIGH DEBT AND NEEDED TO BE ---

Now arrange the circled letters to form the surprise answer, as suggested by the above cartoon.

Print answer here "  " 

PUZZLE 155

WARNING WARNING WARNING WARNING WARNING WARNING WARNING

JUMBLE®

Unscramble these four Jumbles, one letter to each square, to form four ordinary words.

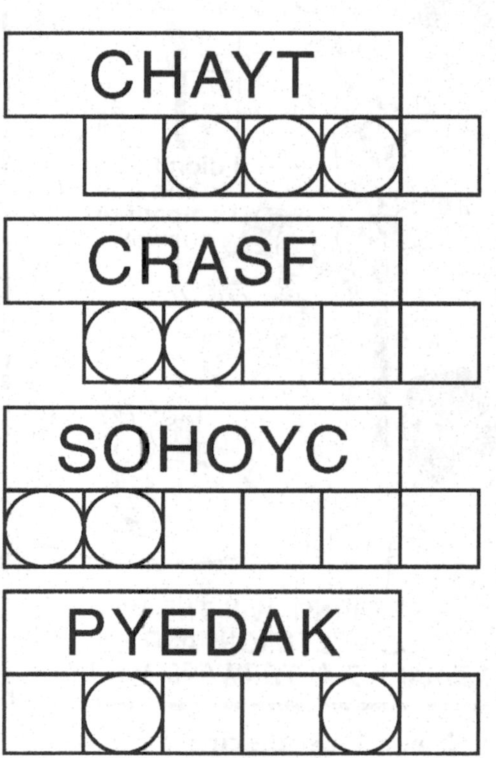
CHAYT
CRASF
SOHOYC
PYEDAK

The tomato cans will be for our vacation this year.
Is there money in this urn or ashes?
THE COUPLE DIDN'T TRUST BANKS AND KEPT THEIR MONEY AT HOME IN THEIR ---

Now arrange the circled letters to form the surprise answer, as suggested by the above cartoon.

Print answer here

PUZZLE 156

WARNING WARNING WARNING WARNING WARNING WARNING WARNING

JUMBLE®

Unscramble these four Jumbles, one letter to each square, to form four ordinary words.

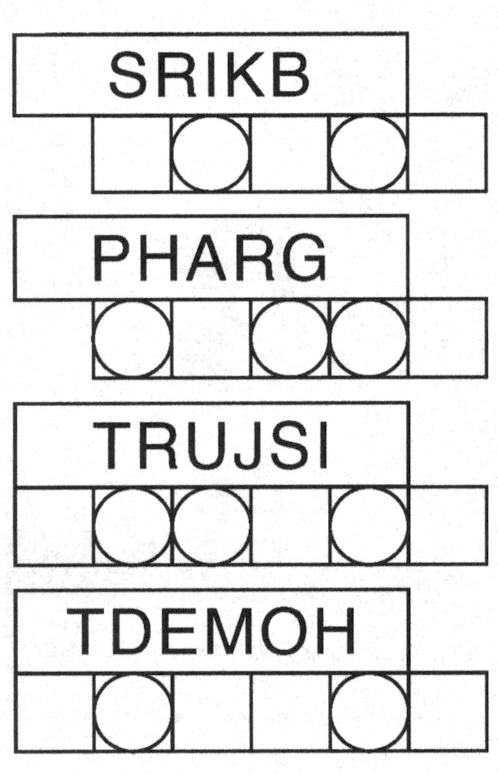

SRIKB
PHARG
TRUJSI
TDEMOH

Thank you, Corkscrew Academy!
Right. It's not like you've talked about it all year.
I didn't want to win this competition anyway.
HE DIDN'T WIN THE WINE COMPETITION, AND HIS REMARKS AFTERWARD WERE ---

Now arrange the circled letters to form the surprise answer, as suggested by the above cartoon.

Print answer here

JUMBLE®

Unscramble these four Jumbles, one letter to each square, to form four ordinary words.

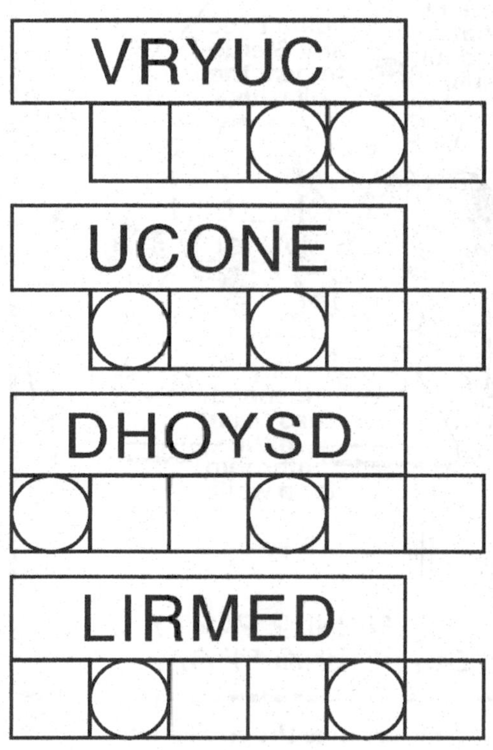
VRYUC
UCONE
DHOYSD
LIRMED

I can't believe the traffic getting here.
It was a nice ride.
DRIVE-IN MOVIE THEATERS WERE POPULAR BECAUSE PEOPLE FLOCKED TO THEM ---

Now arrange the circled letters to form the surprise answer, as suggested by the above cartoon.

Print answer here  

PUZZLE 158

WARNING WARNING WARNING WARNING WARNING WARNING WARNING

JUMBLE®

Unscramble these four Jumbles, one letter to each square, to form four ordinary words.

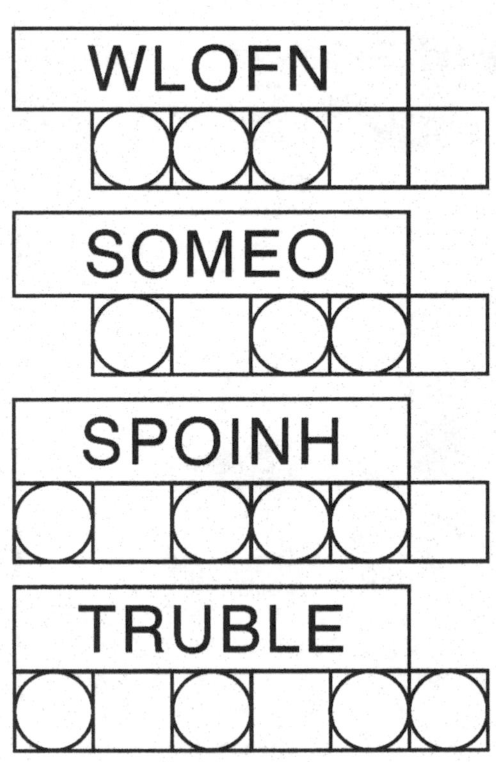

WLOFN
SOMEO
SPOINH
TRUBLE

I can't have peanut oil.
The dog ate the fondue meat.
I didn't see any Sterno to heat the oil with.
My husband has been in the bathroom for a while.
HER DINNER PARTY WAS SUFFERING FROM A ---

Now arrange the circled letters to form the surprise answer, as suggested by the above cartoon.

Print answer here

PUZZLE 159

Unscramble these four Jumbles, one letter to each square, to form four ordinary words.

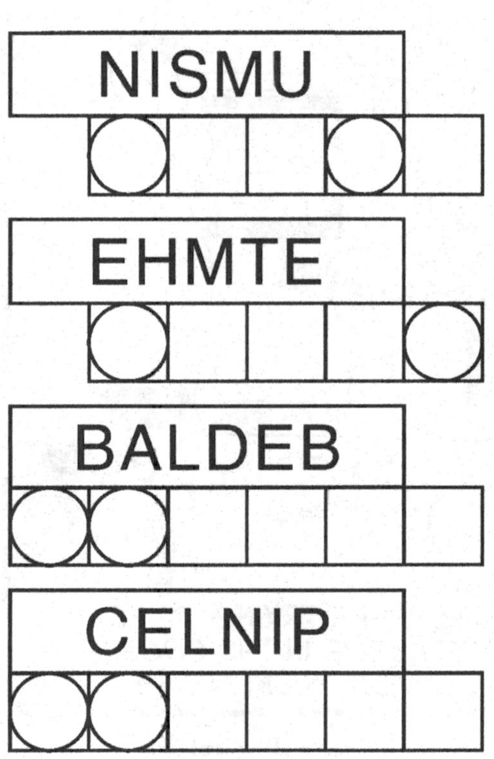
NISMU
EHMTE
BALDEB
CELNIP

Take my hand.
We're almost there!
Great job, everybody!
THE CLIMBERS WHO WORKED TOGETHER IN AN ATTEMPT TO REACH THE SUMMIT ---

Now arrange the circled letters to form the surprise answer, as suggested by the above cartoon.

Print answer here  

WARNING WARNING WARNING WARNING WARNING WARNING WARNING

JUMBLE®

Unscramble these four Jumbles, one letter to each square, to form four ordinary words.

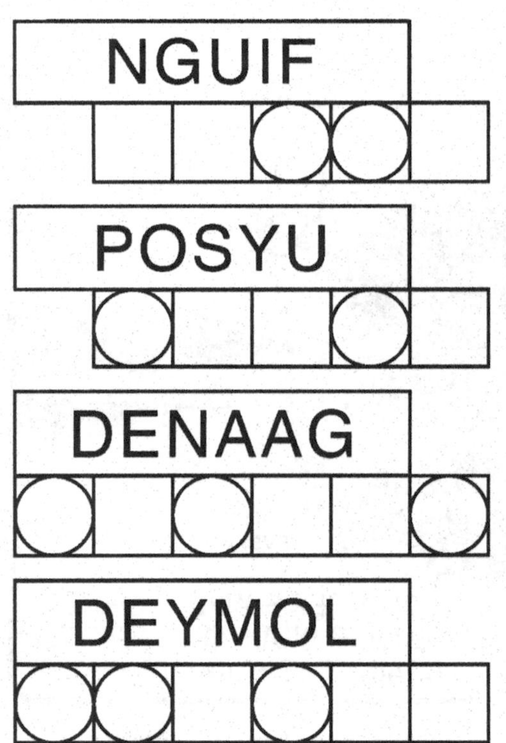
NGUIF
POSYU
DENAAG
DEYMOL

You're not supposed to start the sauce yet.
I thought I'd get it out of the way.
THEY WERE TRYING TO FOLLOW THE RECIPE IN THE COOKBOOK BUT WEREN'T ---

Now arrange the circled letters to form the surprise answer, as suggested by the above cartoon.

Print answer here

 THE  

JUMBLE®
Trouble

Challenger Puzzles

WARNING WARNING WARNING WARNING WARNING WARNING WARNING WARNI

WARNING WARNING WARNING WARNING

JUMBLE®

Unscramble these six Jumbles, one letter to each square, to form six ordinary words.

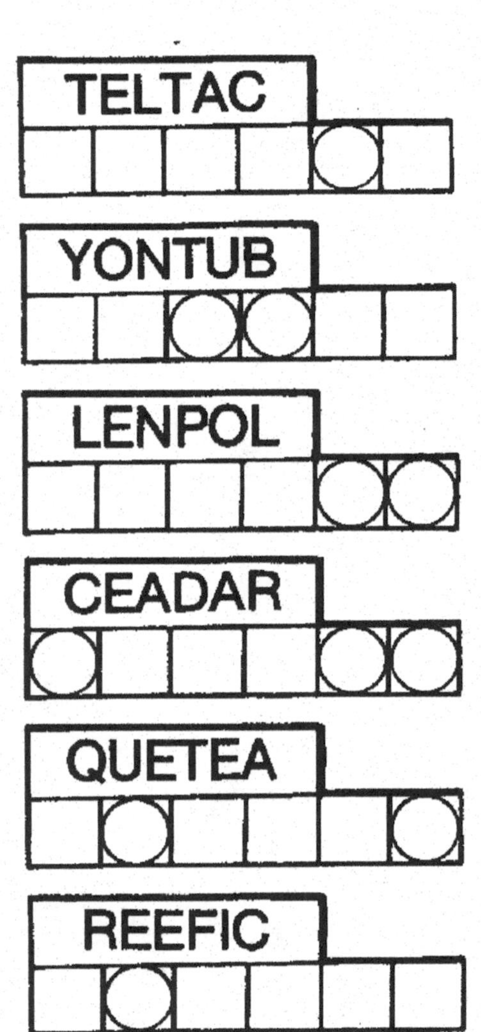
TELTAC
YONTUB
LENPOL
CEADAR
QUETEA
REEFIC

I'll wait until that Roman comes
WHEN CLEOPATRA KEPT SAYING NO, THEY CALLED HER THIS.

Now arrange the circled letters to form the surprise answer, as suggested by the above cartoon.

Print answer here

OF " "

PUZZLE 162

WARNING WARNING WARNING WARNING WARNING WARNING WARNING

JUMBLE®

Unscramble these six Jumbles, one letter to each square, to form six ordinary words.

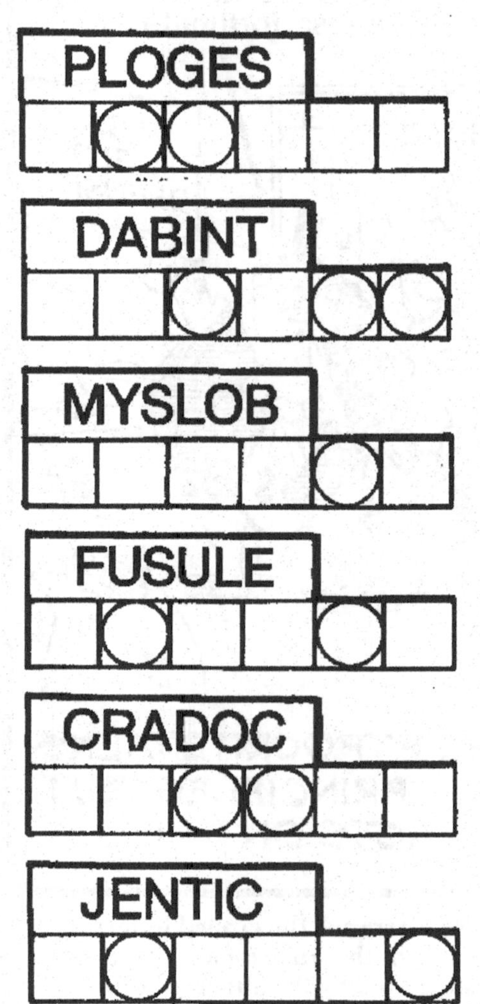

PLOGES
DABINT
MYSLOB
FUSULE
CRADOC
JENTIC

He made a hurried judgment
Should have taken lessons first
HOW SOME SKIERS HAVE BEEN KNOWN TO JUMP.

Now arrange the circled letters to form the surprise answer, as suggested by the above cartoon.

Print answer here

◯◯ "◯◯◯◯◯◯◯◯◯◯"

JUMBLE®

Unscramble these six Jumbles, one letter to each square, to form six ordinary words.

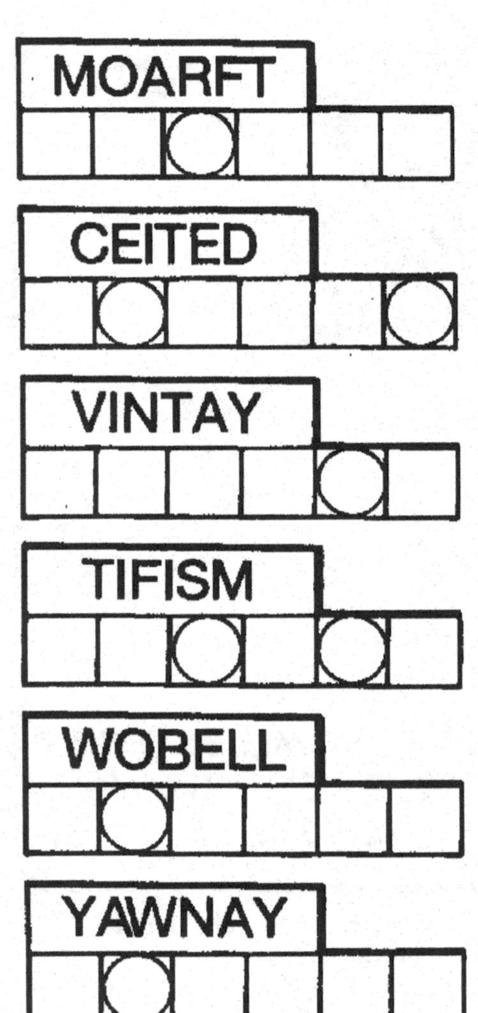
MOARFT
CEITED
VINTAY
TIFISM
WOBELL
YAWNAY

I say that money should be used to help those less fortunate
BANK
HIGH YIELD DEPOSITS
THE HYPOCRITE TALKS ON "PRINCIPLES" BUT ACTS ON THIS.

Now arrange the circled letters to form the surprise answer, as suggested by the above cartoon.

Print answer here

" ◯◯◯◯◯◯◯◯ "

PUZZLE 164

WARNING WARNING WARNING WARNING WARNING WARNING WARNING

JUMBLE®

Unscramble these six Jumbles, one letter to each square, to form six ordinary words.

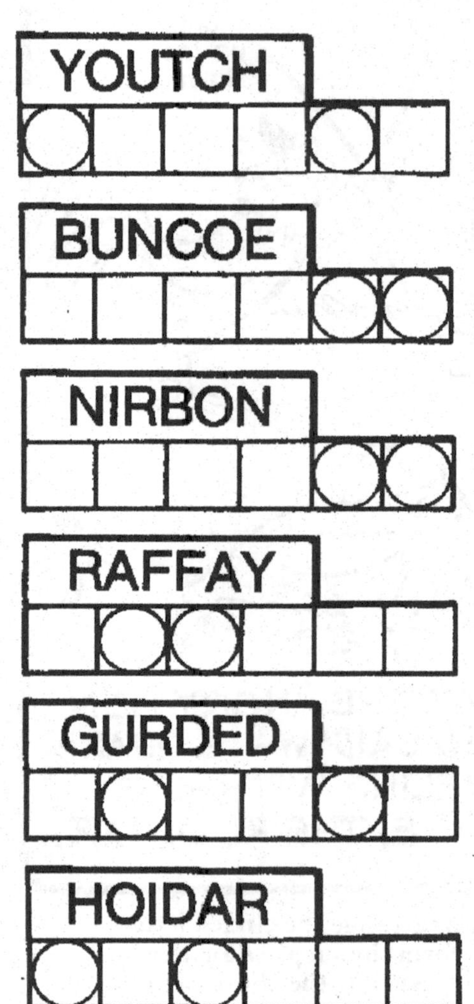

YOUTCH
BUNCOE
NIRBON
RAFFAY
GURDED
HOIDAR

HOW DOES A MONSTER LIKE HIS POTATOES?

Now arrange the circled letters to form the surprise answer, as suggested by the above cartoon.

Print answer here

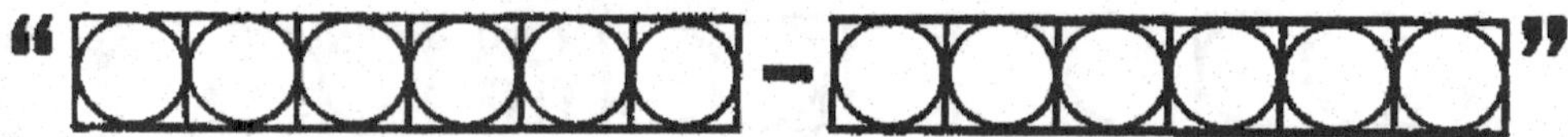

WARNING WARNING WARNING WARNING WARNING WARNING WARNING

PUZZLE 165

JUMBLE®

Unscramble these six Jumbles, one letter to each square, to form six ordinary words.

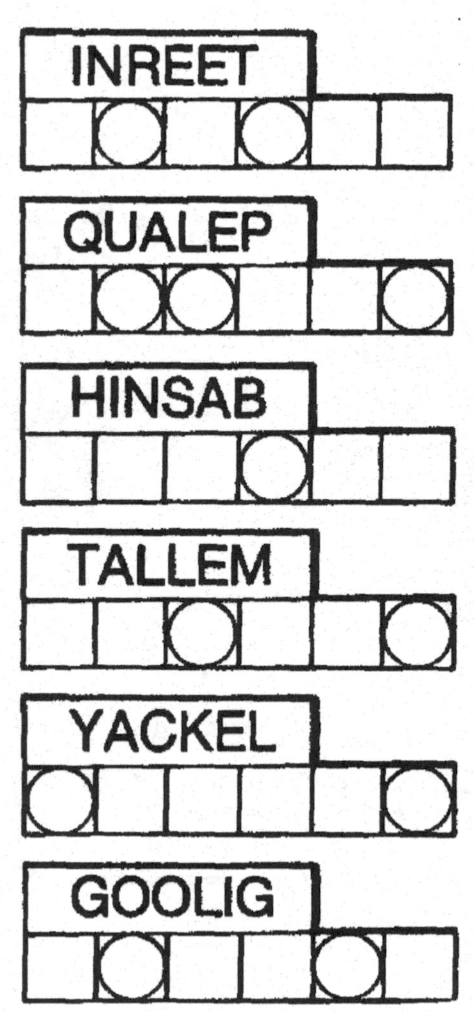
INREET
QUALEP
HINSAB
TALLEM
YACKEL
GOOLIG

I'm giving you an ultimatum, Mr. Wise Guy...
No more late nights on the town
WHAT THE ANGRY HEN ALSO SAID WHILE QUARRELING WITH HER MATE, THE ROOSTER.

Now arrange the circled letters to form the surprise answer, as suggested by the above cartoon.

Print answer here

ON THE !

PUZZLE 166

WARNING WARNING WARNING WARNING WARNING WARNING WARNING

JUMBLE®

Unscramble these six Jumbles, one letter to each square, to form six ordinary words.

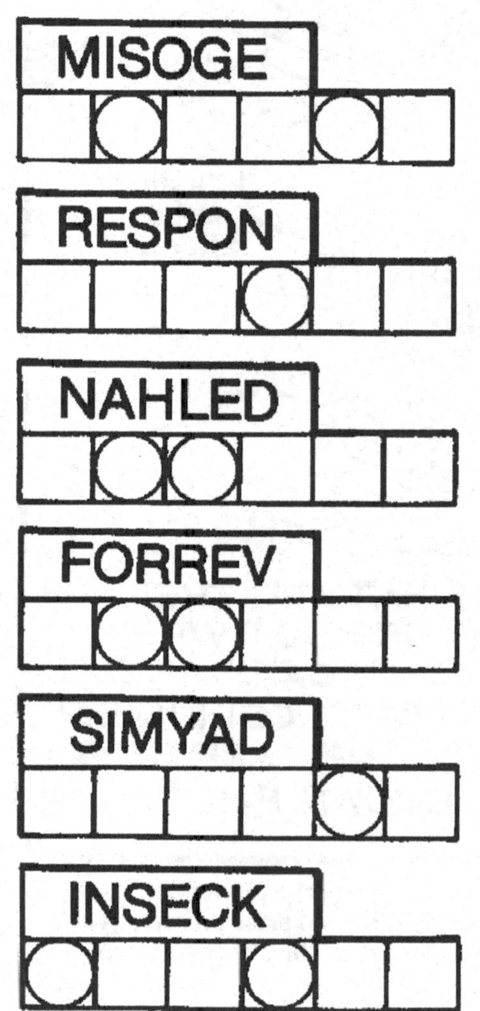
MISOGE
RESPON
NAHLED
FORREV
SIMYAD
INSECK

I wouldn't trust a man who talks out of both sides of his mouth at the same time

WHAT A MAN WHO SPEAKS WITH FORKED TONGUE PROBABLY IS.

Now arrange the circled letters to form the surprise answer, as suggested by the above cartoon.

Print answer here

A
IN THE

WARNING WARNING WARNING WARNING WARNING WARNING WARNING

JUMBLE®

Unscramble these six Jumbles, one letter to each square, to form six ordinary words.

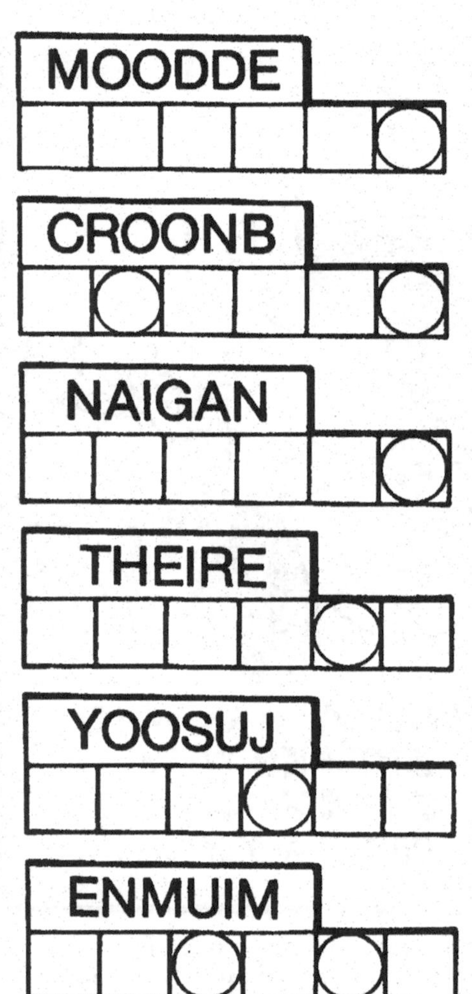
MOODDE
CROONB
NAIGAN
THEIRE
YOOSUJ
ENMUIM

Life ain't so bad after all
WHAT ALL THE SAILORS GOT WHEN A SHIP CARRYING RED PAINT COLLIDED WITH ONE CARRYING BROWN PAINT.

Now arrange the circled letters to form the surprise answer, as suggested by the above cartoon.

Print answer here

“ ”

PUZZLE 168

WARNING WARNING WARNING WARNING WARNING WARNING WARNING

JUMBLE®

Unscramble these six Jumbles, one letter to each square, to form six ordinary words.

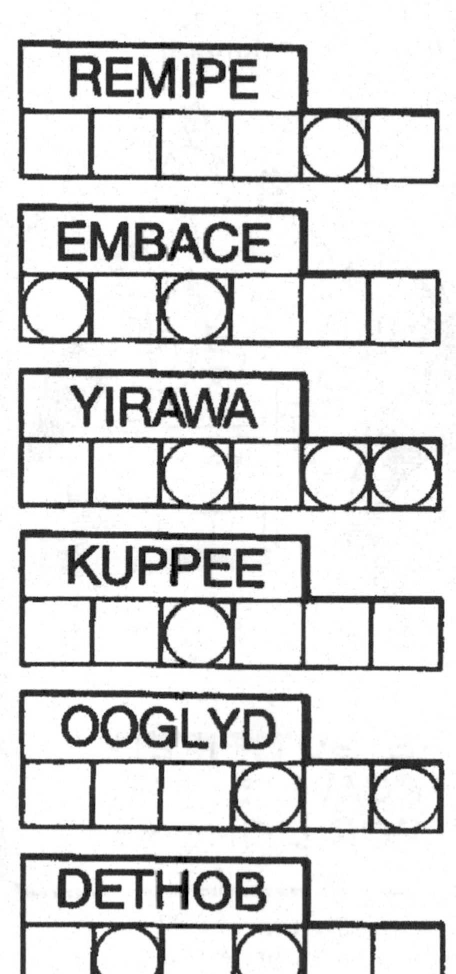
REMIPE
EMBACE
YIRAWA
KUPPEE
OOGLYD
DETHOB

B A
WHAT SHE SANG AFTER SHE CHANGED THE BABY'S DIAPERS.

Now arrange the circled letters to form the surprise answer, as suggested by the above cartoon.

Print answer here

A

PUZZLE 169

WARNING WARNING WARNING WARNING WARNING WARNING WARNING

JUMBLE®

Unscramble these six Jumbles, one letter to each square, to form six ordinary words.

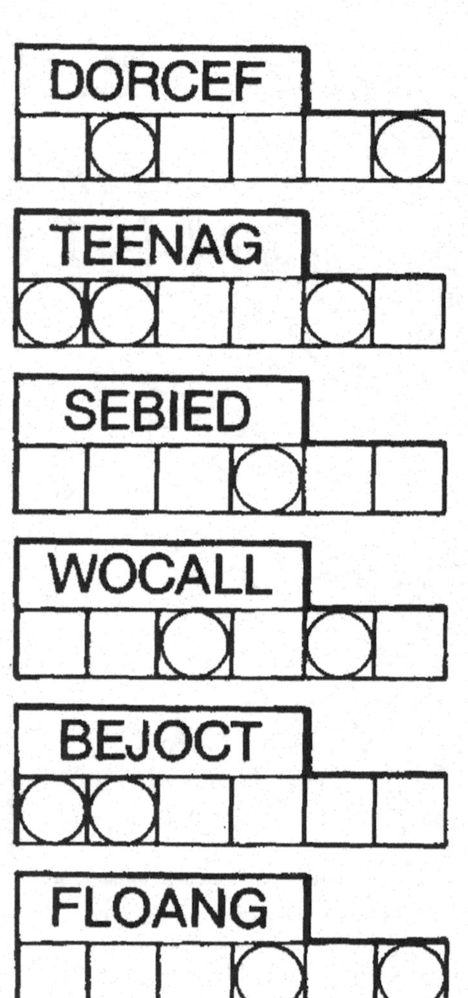
DORCEF
TEENAG
SEBIED
WOCALL
BEJOCT
FLOANG

Had to go to my great-grandmother's funeral
HE GOT FIRED FROM HIS JOB FOR LYING---

Now arrange the circled letters to form the surprise answer, as suggested by the above cartoon.

Print answer here

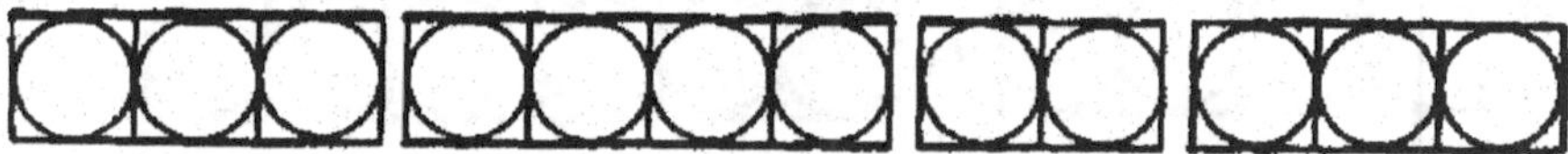

PUZZLE 170

WARNING WARNING WARNING WARNING WARNING WARNING WARNING

JUMBLE®

Unscramble these six Jumbles, one letter to each square, to form six ordinary words.

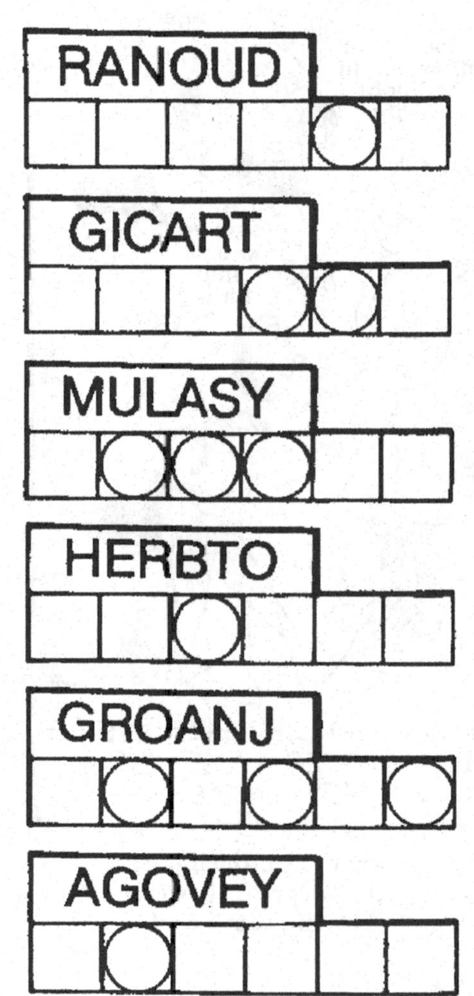
RANOUD
GICART
MULASY
HERBTO
GROANJ
AGOVEY

HIS MOTHER-IN-LAW'S
SHORTCOMING
WAS THIS.

Now arrange the circled letters to form the surprise answer, as suggested by the above cartoon.

Print answer here

HER " ◯◯◯◯ ◯◯◯◯◯◯◯ "

PUZZLE 171

WARNING WARNING WARNING WARNING WARNING WARNING WARNING

JUMBLE®

Unscramble these six Jumbles, one letter to each square, to form six ordinary words.

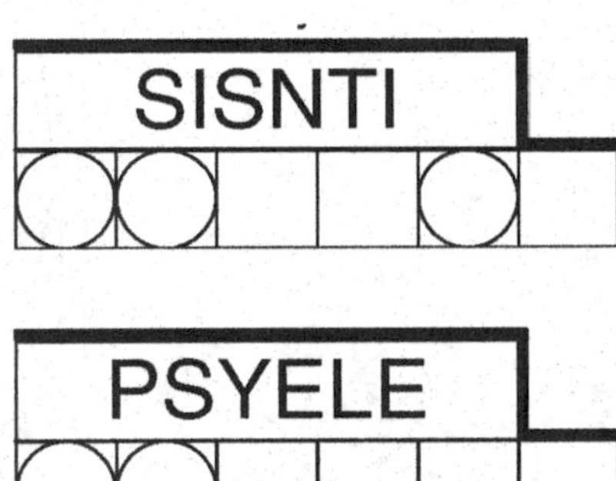

SISNTI
PSYELE

CNATOE

NULEGO

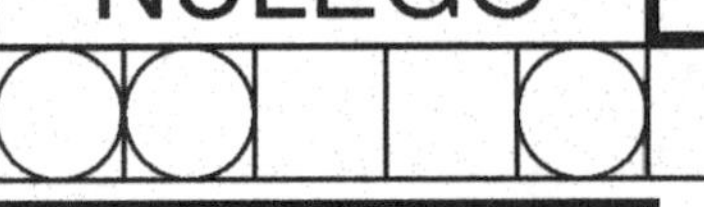

TERAGY

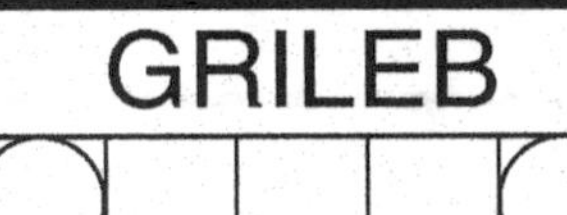

GRILEB

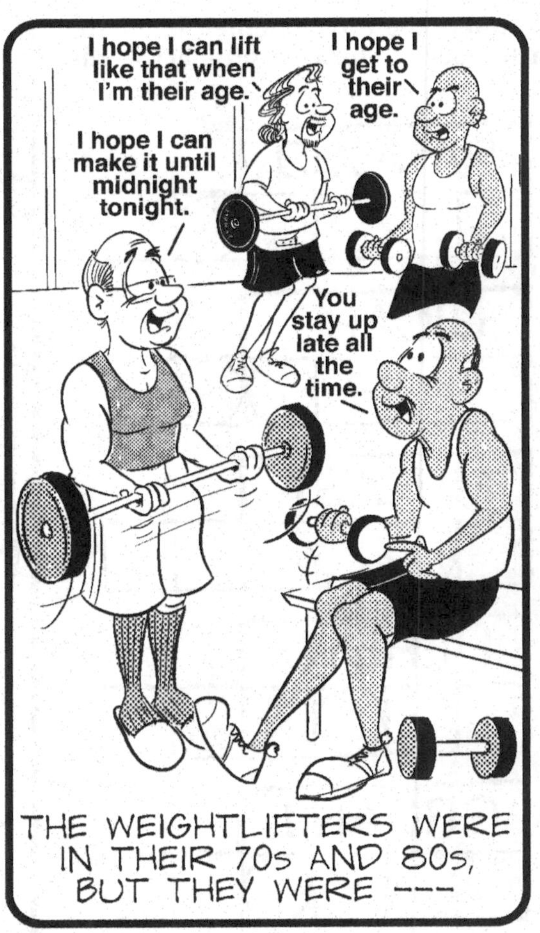

I hope I can lift like that when I'm their age.
I hope I get to their age.
I hope I can make it until midnight tonight.
You stay up late all the time.
THE WEIGHTLIFTERS WERE IN THEIR 70s AND 80s, BUT THEY WERE ---

Now arrange the circled letters to form the surprise answer, as suggested by the above cartoon.

Print answer here

PUZZLE
172

WARNING WARNING WARNING WARNING WARNING WARNING WARNING

JUMBLE®

Unscramble these six Jumbles, one letter to each square, to form six ordinary words.

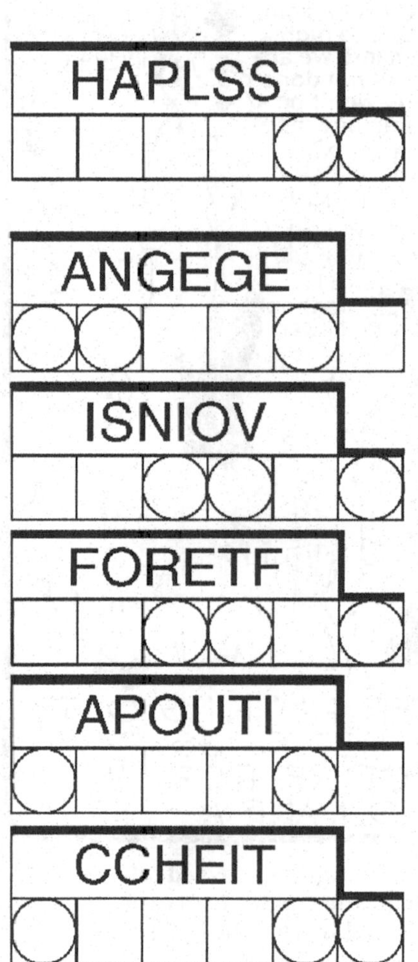
HAPLSS
ANGEGE
ISNIOV
FORETF
APOUTI
CCHEIT

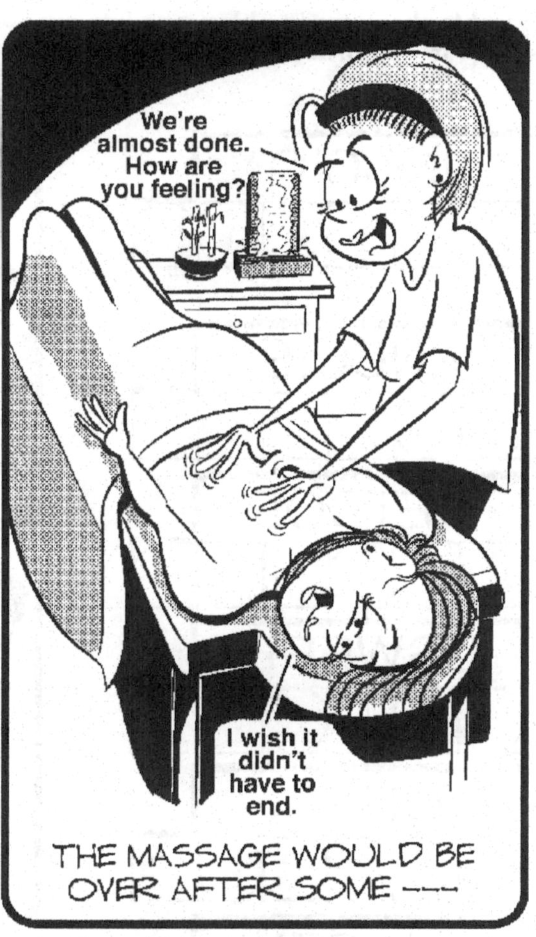
We're almost done. How are you feeling?
I wish it didn't have to end.
THE MASSAGE WOULD BE OVER AFTER SOME ---

Now arrange the circled letters to form the surprise answer, as suggested by the above cartoon.

Print answer here

JUMBLE®

Unscramble these six Jumbles, one letter to each square, to form six ordinary words.

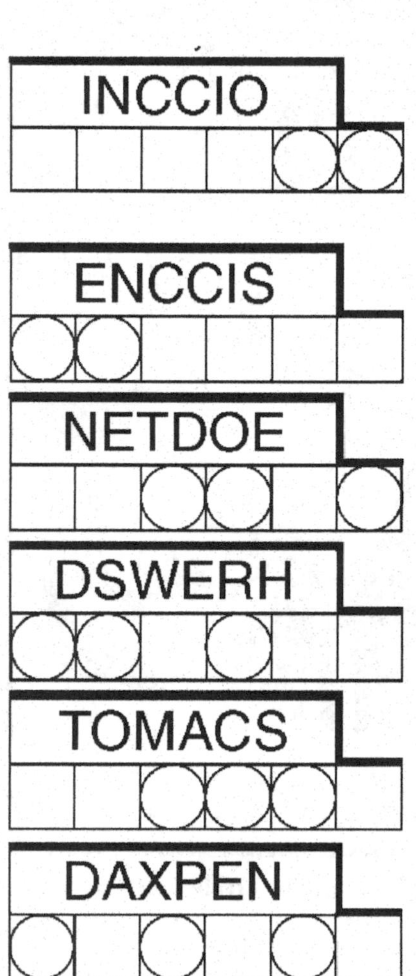
INCCIO
ENCCIS
NETDOE
DSWERH
TOMACS
DAXPEN

I have an announcement. Due to high demand, we are out of hot dogs. We won't be getting any more.
FULL COURT CAFE
BURGERS $12
HOT DOG $7
POPCORN $5
NACHOS $8
I like nachos better.
AFTER RUNNING OUT OF HOT DOGS, THE FOOD VENDOR HAD TO MAKE A ---

Now arrange the circled letters to form the surprise answer, as suggested by the above cartoon.

Print answer here

PUZZLE
174

WARNING WARNING WARNING WARNING WARNING WARNING WARNING

JUMBLE®

Unscramble these six Jumbles, one letter to each square, to form six ordinary words.

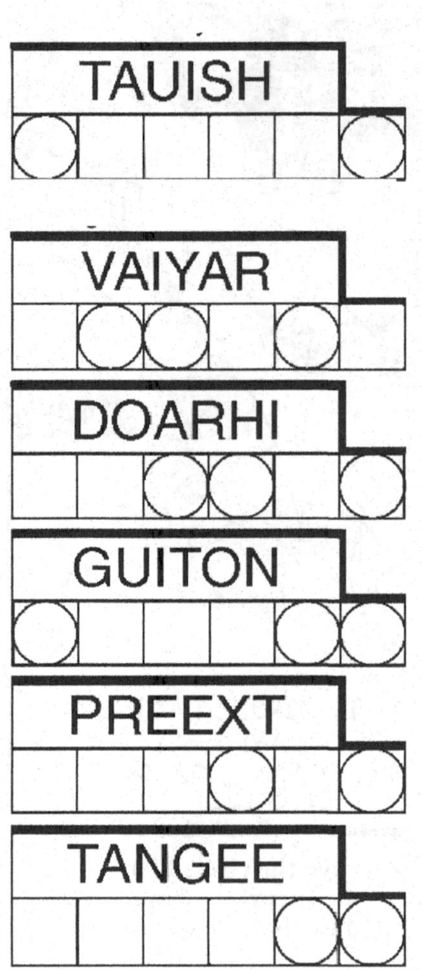

TAUISH
VAIYAR
DOARHI
GUITON
PREEXT
TANGEE

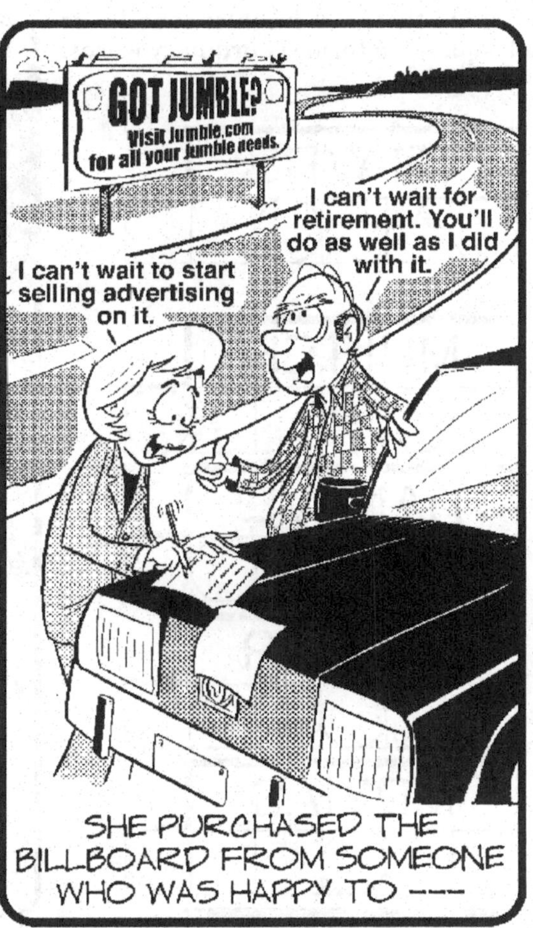

GOT JUMBLE?
Visit Jumble.com for all your Jumble needs.
I can't wait for retirement. You'll do as well as I did with it.
I can't wait to start selling advertising on it.
SHE PURCHASED THE BILLBOARD FROM SOMEONE WHO WAS HAPPY TO ---

Now arrange the circled letters to form the surprise answer, as suggested by the above cartoon.

Print answer here

PUZZLE 175

WARNING WARNING WARNING WARNING WARNING WARNING WARNING

JUMBLE®

Unscramble these six Jumbles, one letter to each square, to form six ordinary words.

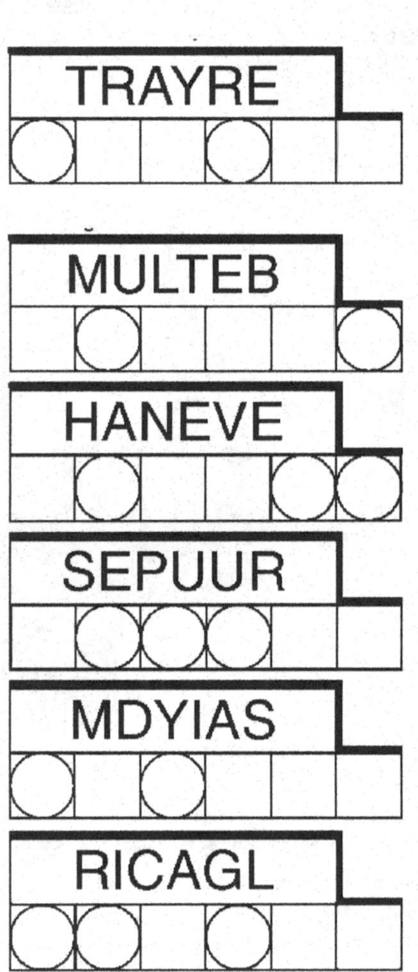

TRAYRE
MULTEB
HANEVE
SEPUUR
MDYIAS
RICAGL

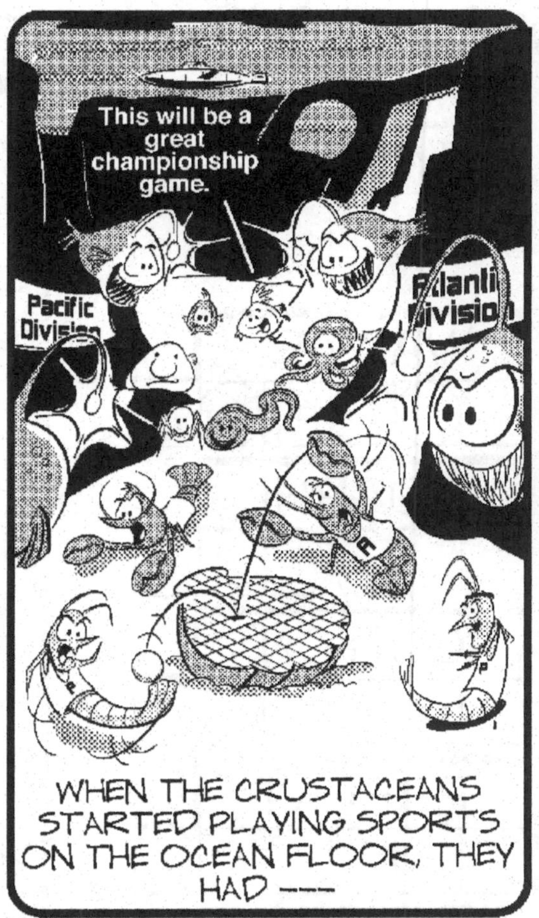

This will be a great championship game.
Pacific Division
Atlanti Divisio
WHEN THE CRUSTACEANS STARTED PLAYING SPORTS ON THE OCEAN FLOOR, THEY HAD ---

Now arrange the circled letters to form the surprise answer, as suggested by the above cartoon.

Print answer here

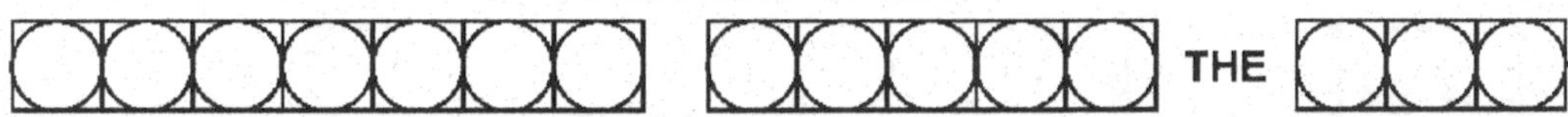

THE

PUZZLE 176

WARNING WARNING WARNING WARNING WARNING WARNING WARNING

JUMBLE®

Unscramble these six Jumbles, one letter to each square, to form six ordinary words.

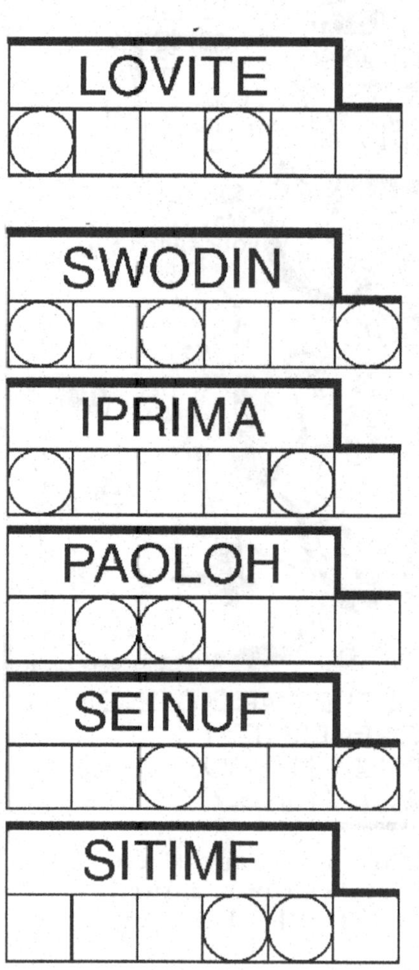

LOVITE
SWODIN
IPRIMA
PAOLOH
SEINUF
SITIMF

I don't even need binoculars from here!
What a view!
WITH SEATS IN THE FRONT ROW ON THE 50-YARD LINE, THEY HAD A GREAT ---

Now arrange the circled letters to form the surprise answer, as suggested by the above cartoon.

Print answer here

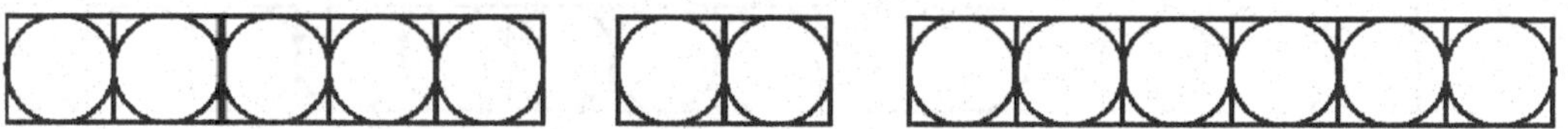

PUZZLE 177

WARNING WARNING WARNING WARNING WARNING WARNING WARNING

JUMBLE®

Unscramble these six Jumbles, one letter to each square, to form six ordinary words.

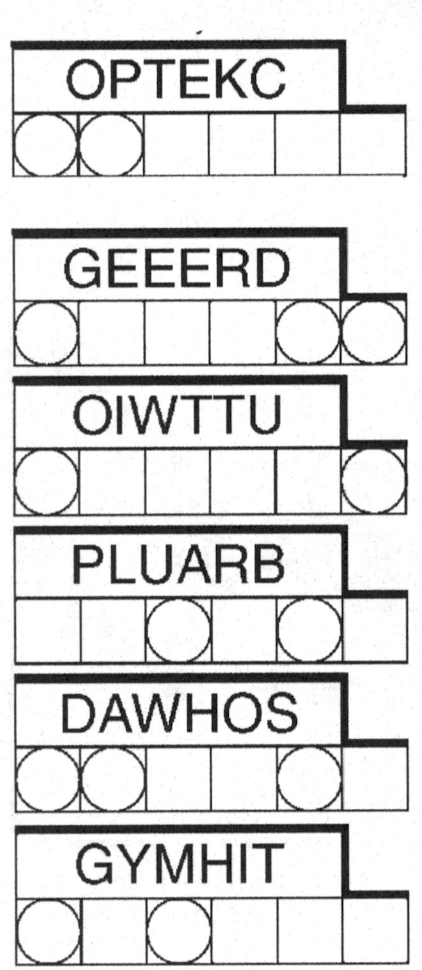

OPTEKC
GEEERD
OIWTTU
PLUARB
DAWHOS
GYMHIT

What do you think?
I love the vibe here.
May I take your climate helmet?
Wow!

WHEN THE MARS COLONY OPENED ITS FIRST RESTAURANT, CUSTOMERS REALLY LIKED ITS ---

Now arrange the circled letters to form the surprise answer, as suggested by the above cartoon.

Print answer here

PUZZLE
178

WARNING WARNING WARNING WARNING WARNING WARNING WARNING

JUMBLE®

Unscramble these six Jumbles, one letter to each square, to form six ordinary words.

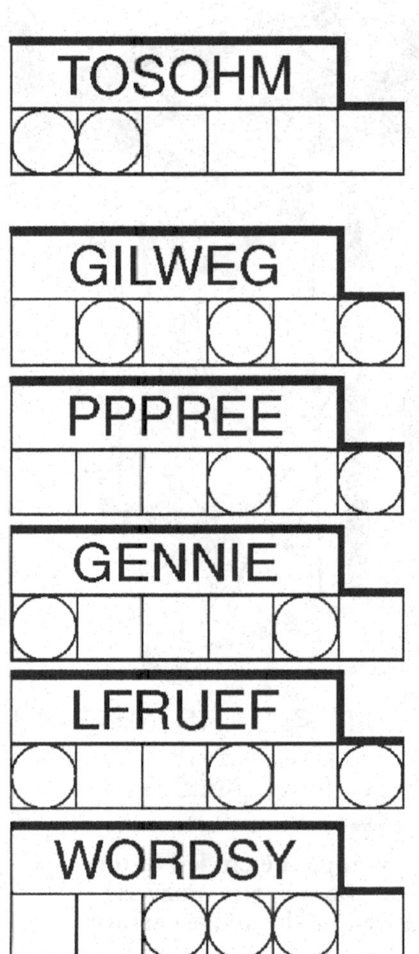

TOSOHM
GILWEG
PPPREE
GENNIE
LFRUEF
WORDSY

We need a raise and benefits!
If we don't get all of our demands, we'll strike!
We need new brooms!
I need a new mop!

THE JANITORS' UNION WANTED TO MAKE CHANGES AND WAS ASKING FOR ---

Now arrange the circled letters to form the surprise answer, as suggested by the above cartoon.

Print answer here

JUMBLE®

Unscramble these six Jumbles, one letter to each square, to form six ordinary words.

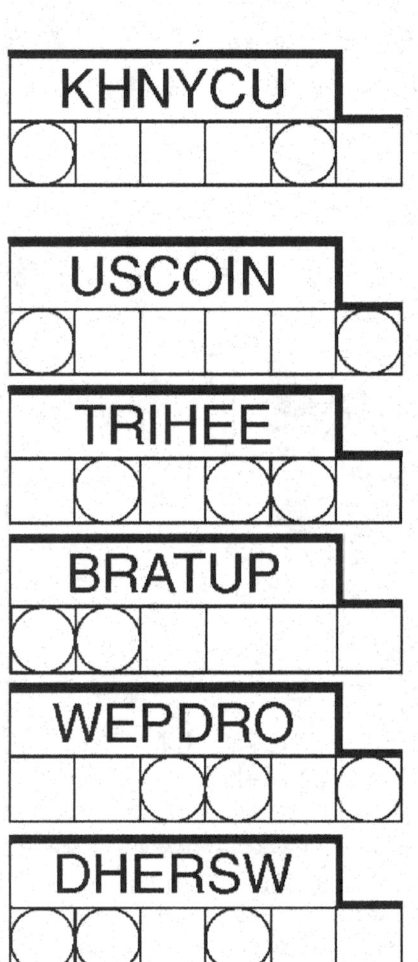
KHNYCU
USCOIN
TRIHEE
BRATUP
WEPDRO
DHERSW

Are you okay?
Ow! I just tweaked something!
THE CAR REPAIRS WERE GOING WELL UNTIL THE AUTO MECHANIC ---

Now arrange the circled letters to form the surprise answer, as suggested by the above cartoon.

Print answer here

PUZZLE 180

WARNING WARNING WARNING WARNING WARNING WARNING WARNING

JUMBLE®

Unscramble these six Jumbles, one letter to each square, to form six ordinary words.

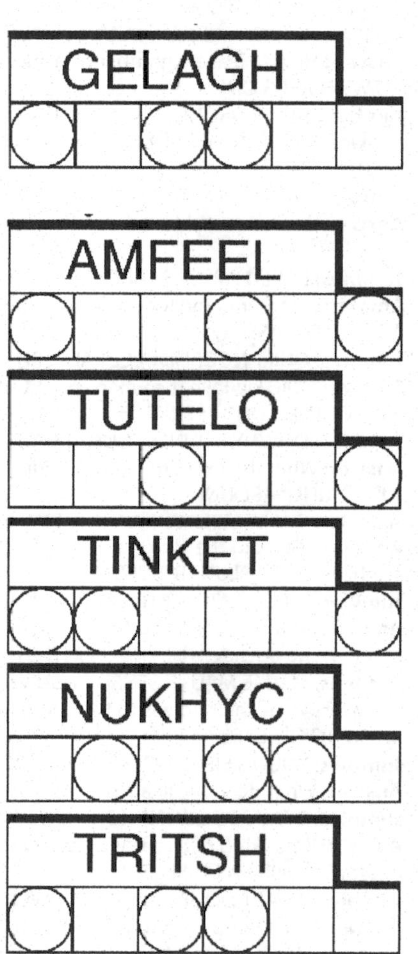
GELAGH
AMFEEL
TUTELO
TINKET
NUKHYC
TRITSH

Greetings!
Better late than never, Sir Roger.
Here come my regulars.
THE MEDIEVAL TAVERN WAS OPEN DAILY UNTIL 12 A.M. AND SERVED CUSTOMERS ---

Now arrange the circled letters to form the surprise answer, as suggested by the above cartoon.

Print answer here

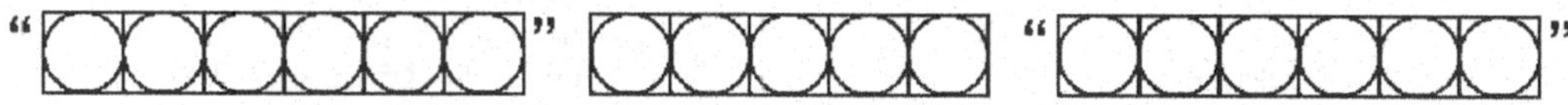

Answers

1. **Jumbles:** MOUSY CHUTE INTONE BROGUE
Answer: What you might get from one hug—ENOUGH
2. **Jumbles:** BUMPY WHISK CUDDLE FATHOM
Answer: That hobo was down and out but not exactly this—"WASHED-UP"
3. **Jumbles:** ERUPT TEMPO PURITY CLOVEN
Answer: Would you say that the kid who ate too many hot dogs was suffering from this?—"PUPPY" LOVE
4. **Jumbles:** APPLY BURLY EFFIGY PONDER
Answer: How some honest opinions are expressed—OPENLY
5. **Jumbles:** AGILE CABIN FESTAL COHORT
Answer: They named their team the Spiders because all of them knew how to do this—CATCH FLIES
6. **Jumbles:** AGENT HOBBY IMPUTE DROWSY
Answer: What that undercover agent was also known as—A SPY IN BED
7. **Jumbles:** SHINY FANCY EMBODY UNLESS
Answer: What he said when a man arrived with a package marked "C.O.D"—SOUNDS FISHY
8. **Jumbles:** ADMIT ROBIN STUCCO JUNGLE
Answer: "This coffee tastes like mud!"—"IT WAS JUST 'GROUND'"
9. **Jumbles:** AGONY GAMUT MASCOT POLISH
Answer: The hypochondriac said he was so sick he couldn't even do this—COMPLAIN
10. **Jumbles:** SYNOD CAKED KETTLE ANYHOW
Answer: Every dog has its "day" except one with a sore tail which has this—ITS "WEAK END"
11. **Jumbles:** RAVEN GUMBO LEVITY CUDGEL
Answer: How they knew that the man-eating shark had been shot dead—THERE WAS A "BULLET-IN"
12. **Jumbles:** TASTY PARKA OBLIGE DOUBLE
Answer: Why the shopkeeper said farewell to that bargain merchandise—IT WAS "A GOOD BUY"
13. **Jumbles:** UNCLE TOPAZ ORPHAN SOLACE
Answer: That dumbbell was planning to put his feet into the oven in order to do this—POP HIS CORNS
14. **Jumbles:** STOKE IMPEL BALLET CANKER
Answer: He is wearing a nice new suit but his dog only this—"PANTS"
15. **Jumbles:** IRONY AUDIT DEVICE GUNNER
Answer: He hated to take his car out in such weather, although they called it this—A "DRIVING" RAIN
16. **Jumbles:** TEASE FAIRY TROPHY NICETY
Answer: The little baseball player decided to become a Boy Scout so he could learn to do this—"PITCH" A TENT
17. **Jumbles:** RIGOR ANKLE TROUGH HITHER
Answer: Why thermometer sales are always held in cold weather—WHEN IT'S HOT, THEY'RE HIGHER
18. **Jumbles:** WHOSE ALIVE BALSAM LICHEN
Answer: What they couldn't figure out when the X-ray technician introduced her new boyfriend—WHAT SHE SAW IN HIM
19. **Jumbles:** LYING PRIOR TEMPER DEPUTY
Answer: He didn't speak to his wife for a whole week because he didn't want to do this—INTERRUPT
20. **Jumbles:** PILOT OFTEN YELLOW EULOGY
Answer: A guy slapped him on the back and then asked him this—HOW'RE YOU "PEELING"?
21. **Jumbles:** LYRIC UTTER PENMAN CODGER
Answer: Would they be playing this?—RAGTIME
22. **Jumbles:** BLOOD TWILL MALTED LAVISH
Answer: "This soup tastes like dishwater!"—"HOW CAN YOU TELL?"
23. **Jumbles:** BLAZE AWFUL LETHAL FROTHY
Answer: Whatever he claimed to "stand for," his audience wouldn't do this—"FALL FOR"
24. **Jumbles:** TOXIC GNOME CONCUR ORATOR
Answer: What the countess said her husband was—A "NO-ACCOUNT"
25. **Jumbles:** BEFIT MUSTY VACUUM EXHALE
Answer: What the I.R.S. called the new levy on hitchhikers—THE THUMB "TAX"
26. **Jumbles:** PUPPY VENOM ERMINE FLATLY
Answer: Baby was mother's little this—"YELPER"
27. **Jumbles:** GLAND LEAVE NOVICE RELISH
Answer: Why is an empty purse always the same?—NEVER ANY CHANGE IN IT
28. **Jumbles:** ACUTE FORGO BURLAP GAINED
Answer: Would the guard at a hat factory carry this?—A CAP GUN
29. **Jumbles:** TWEAK POPPY SALUTE NEWEST
Answer: That veteran comedian knows a good gag when he does this—STEALS ONE
30. **Jumbles:** COUGH MIDGE GOVERN BODILY
Answer: How to leave a gambling casino with a small fortune—GO WITH A BIG ONE
31. **Jumbles:** ALTAR DRONE LUNACY FOURTH
Answer: What you've got when you stand with your back to the fireplace—A COLD FRONT
32. **Jumbles:** TAKEN JOINT TYPHUS GROTTO
Answer: What she said to the invisible man—YOU'RE OUTTA SIGHT
33. **Jumbles:** BAKED ABYSS SATIRE PRISON
Answer: Another name for the "poor fish" who landed in jail—A STRIPED "BASS"
34. **Jumbles:** QUILT NOOSE DULCET SUPERB
Answer: "Will you love me when I'm old and ugly?"—"OF COURSE, I DO"
35. **Jumbles:** DOWNY BOUND NOUGAT RATHER
Answer: What the executioner did during a slack period—JUST "HUNG" AROUND
36. **Jumbles:** CRAZE VIPER SINFUL KNOTTY
Answer: What did the astronauts call those insects they found on the moon?—"LUNAR-TICKS"
37. **Jumbles:** JOUST PATIO OUTLET KERNEL
Answer: What the cops said they would do when a hole was found in the outside wall—LOOK INTO IT
38. **Jumbles:** PLUME MAUVE STURDY COUSIN
Answer: When she said yes to the composer it was this—MUSIC TO HIS EARS
39. **Jumbles:** YOUNG SIEGE GOODLY OBLONG
Answer: What do you call a wet pup?—A SOGGY DOGGY
40. **Jumbles:** EXACT BOGUS SIPHON REALTY
Answer: What kind of a career did that crooked sculptor carve out for himself—A CHISELER'S
41. **Jumbles:** ADAPT DOUBT WISELY PLOWED
Answer: What happened to those "paper" profits he supposedly earned?—THEY BLEW AWAY
42. **Jumbles:** WOVEN BLIMP EFFORT POORLY
Answer: What you are when you have something on the boss—"FIRE PROOF"
43. **Jumbles:** ELUDE QUAKE STUPID IMPOSE
Answer: What the garbageman said he was—AT HER "DISPOSAL"
44. **Jumbles:** MIRTH SWISH HEIFER BIGAMY
Answer: How to find out if your watch is gaining—WEIGH IT
45. **Jumbles:** ELITE FELON TRYING LAUNCH
Answer: When he finally got the fireplace working, she was this—"GRATE-FULL"

46. **Jumbles:** SHAKY ANNOY COSTLY ENDURE
Answer: What that old hot rod was—A "SHOT" ROD

47. **Jumbles:** BATHE HIKER SMUDGE POROUS
Answer: When the cowboys finished branding them, the cows were really this—"IMPRESSED"

48. **Jumbles:** HEAVY JOLLY NESTLE BEGONE
Answer: What kind of an environment did he try to establish for his family?—A "STABLE" ONE

49. **Jumbles:** PYLON CHAFE BUCKLE FIDDLE
Answer: What barbed wire was first used for—"DE FENCE"

50. **Jumbles:** COVEY ELDER NOBODY APPALL
Answer: What was the expression on that zombie's face?—"DEAD PAN"

51. **Jumbles:** CHALK YEARN INVADE RADIUS
Answer: What happened to the missing can of shellac?—IT "VARNISHED"

52. **Jumbles:** DOUGH VOCAL PESTLE HERMIT
Answer: What the pup who loved getting washed must have been—A "SHAMPOODLE"

53. **Jumbles:** GUILE PLAIT KENNEL IMPACT
Answer: What a wrinkle is—THE "NICK" OF TIME

54. **Jumbles:** PIETY CHIDE LAWFUL NOODLE
Answer: Why the cat went to see the vet—HE WAS "FELINE" LOW (feeling low)

55. **Jumbles:** MANGE ACRID BUTTON CHOSEN
Answer: Why the inventor of fishhooks became a millionaire—THEY REALLY "CAUGHT ON"

56. **Jumbles:** ABOVE ENACT WEASEL FLUNKY
Answer: What the cowboys were hoping to get out of the rodeo—A FEW BUCKS

57. **Jumbles:** WIPED BATON NINETY GALAXY
Answer: What to give your wife at 3 a.m.—AN EXPLANATION

58. **Jumbles:** EPOCH GUARD BASKET CACTUS
Answer: What the compulsive golfer was—A "CRACKPUTT"

59. **Jumbles:** FRIAR MERCY WALNUT INVENT
Answer: That executive shake-up amounted to this—A "TITLE" WAVE

60. **Jumbles:** FLOOD KNIFE PULPIT DECEIT
Answer: Hints are often dropped but seldom this—PICKED UP

61. **Jumbles:** RIVET NEWLY WIDEST FAMISH
Answer: He committed a traffic violation when he was driving under the influence of this—HIS WIFE

62. **Jumbles:** ENEMY BORAX GIBLET KIMONO
Answer: Thinks he's "going places," when he's really this—BEING "TAKEN"

63. **Jumbles:** LOVER JUICY GIGOLO NOTIFY
Answer: What that short guy said while proposing—I "LONG" FOR YOU

64. **Jumbles:** FLAME LIBEL STICKY PERSON
Answer: What you'd expect a good tongue sandwich to do—SPEAK FOR ITSELF

65. **Jumbles:** MOUNT OPERA CANDID SUBWAY
Answer: What he said when the judge sentenced him to be hanged—THAT'S BAD "NOOSE"

66. **Jumbles:** DRAFT HONEY TRICKY WALRUS
Answer: They invited that screwball painter because he was always this—THE LIFE OF THE "ARTY"

67. **Jumbles:** COWER DAUNT JOYOUS BISHOP
Answer: He knew how to make extra money with his shovel by being good at this—SNOW JOBS

68. **Jumbles:** IDIOT PERKY NAUGHT FUSION
Answer: What a dictionary that stops at nothing must be—UNFINISHED

69. **Jumbles:** JUDGE QUASH BLAZER CHARGE
Answer: Something you get by using it—"A HEAD"

70. **Jumbles:** BELIE CIVIL EXTENT SCHOOL
Answer: What alcohol causes people to give when they lose their inhibitions—EXHIBITIONS

71. **Jumbles:** DITTO ANNUL THRUSH ENTAIL
Answer: "Tact" is what some people have while others do this—TELL THE TRUTH

72. **Jumbles:** TWEET CURIO FORGOT SLOGAN
Answer: Why they fired some of those chickens from the farm team—TOO MANY "FOWLS"

73. **Jumbles:** BERET FUSSY TWINGE MADMAN
Answer: Go to them for help when you're attacked by annoying insects—THE "SWAT" TEAM

74. **Jumbles:** FEIGN NIPPY MORGUE SLOUCH
Answer: He gave up trying to learn wrestling because he couldn't get this—A GRIP ON HIMSELF

75. **Jumbles:** CAPON FENCE NUTRIA BEADLE
Answer: Although he didn't eat a thing at dinner, he was this—"FED UP"

76. **Jumbles:** HENCE SNACK EMBARK COWARD
Answer: "When did you first notice that weak back?"—"A WEEK BACK"

77. **Jumbles:** ROUSE FAMED GROUCH DONKEY
Answer: The baker left his job because he didn't this—"KNEAD" THE DOUGH

78. **Jumbles:** DIRTY BAGGY GUIDED ANSWER
Answer: What do you get when a fat man marries a fat lady?—A BIG WEDDING

79. **Jumbles:** LEECH JUROR MOTIVE BELFRY
Answer: What you might expect him to do when she spends all that money on some silly art object—OBJECT

80. **Jumbles:** POISE HITCH DEMISE EYEFUL
Answer: What's a mermaid?—A "DEEP-SHE FISH"

81. **Jumbles:** GLITZ GRILL TRENCH TATTLE
Answer: They wanted to install a new traffic signal and just needed the city to—GREEN LIGHT IT

82. **Jumbles:** KAZOO BLINK CRUTCH SPRAWL
Answer: Construction of the railroad would fall behind schedule if they didn't get—BACK ON TRACK

83. **Jumbles:** FAINT CAGEY SLICED LOUNGE
Answer: The Frisbee golf course was closing. The couple played to have—ONE LAST FLING

84. **Jumbles:** DRINK FLASH FORMAT BUTTON
Answer: He wanted a soft mattress. She didn't and was going to—STAND FIRM

85. **Jumbles:** MUMMY STAND POETIC FREELY
Answer: Clocks didn't go digital until—MODERN TIMES

86. **Jumbles:** DOILY FEWER SHROUD TOMATO
Answer: Everyone who saw the moon landing on TV thought it was—OUT OF THIS WORLD

87. **Jumbles:** LUNGE TIGER PONCHO CHANCE
Answer: Because of a drought, the pumpkin farmers were going through a—ROUGH PATCH

88. **Jumbles:** PRIZE ORBIT RODENT FUNGUS
Answer: They'd gotten a $70 parking ticket, and now he was reading the—FINE PRINT

89. **Jumbles:** ALIAS TUNER INTACT UTMOST
Answer: The campsites being smaller than expected resulted in a—"TENTS" SITUATION

90. **Jumbles:** ALLOW CRIMP PERSON AGENDA
Answer: The Wright Brothers' approach to aviation was—"PLANE" AND SIMPLE

91. **Jumbles:** JOUST AHEAD POROUS SNAPPY
Answer: The hyphen liked adding pepper to his food, but—JUST A DASH

92. **Jumbles:** IRONY DEPTH STORMY INVENT
Answer: The possibility that ESP was real didn't even—ENTER HIS MIND

93. **Jumbles:** PRONE SILKY STRAND DIVIDE
Answer: The ghosts got along so well because they were—KINDRED SPIRITS

94. **Jumbles:** OFTEN MADLY VIOLIN ZIPPER
Answer: When taking photos of Chuck Yeager breaking the sound barrier, it was tough to—ZOOM IN

95. **Jumbles:** EVOKE VIGIL DISMAL KNIGHT
Answer: When people visit Graceland, they get to see how Elvis—LIVED LIKE A KING

96. **Jumbles:** BEACH YOUNG ROTARY FOLKSY
Answer: The handyman spent so much on advertising because he wanted to—GO FOR BROKE

97. **Jumbles:** GAVEL SENSE SUBMIT WIZARD
Answer: When the boxer surprised her with a marriage proposal, she had a—"RING-SIDE" SEAT

98. **Jumbles:** BISON CELLO GEYSER DEARLY
Answer: The effort Auguste Rodin put into his sculpture "The Thinker," was—"CONSIDER-ABLE"

99. **Jumbles:** GRAFT BURLY KNOTTY UNEASY
Answer: The dog's favorite type of chair is a—"BARK-A-LOUNGER"

100. **Jumbles:** FLAIL COVET SHRUNK MORALE
Answer: The company manufactured clown shoes, which was—NO SMALL "FEET"

101. **Jumbles:** VALID CLIMB POLICY SHRILL
Answer: Directing the third-graders' stage performance was tough and certainly not—CHILD'S PLAY

102. **Jumbles:** GOOSE RAYON MIFFED ENTITY
Answer: They were taking a tour on horseback, which would start—"RIDE" ON TIME

103. **Jumbles:** OFTEN KHAKI PEOPLE SCENIC
Answer: For the pool shark, it was like stealing money, thanks to his ability to—PICK POCKETS

104. **Jumbles:** STRUM PLUSH UPBEAT ENTICE
Answer: When it comes to winning money playing blackjack, it's hard to—TURN THE TABLES

105. **Jumbles:** HUSKY OLDER HUBCAP PALLET
Answer: She opened her store in a busy neighborhood. Now She needed customers to—STOP "BUY"

106. **Jumbles:** TANGY LIMIT KOSHER CRANNY
Answer: They'd had some thefts at the bowling alley and worried the thief might—STRIKE AGAIN

107. **Jumbles:** PETTY TOXIC IODINE JAGUAR
Answer: When Billy dared his buddy to jump the fence, he was trying to—"GOAT" HIM INTO IT

108. **Jumbles:** CLOAK PERCH HARDEN ENTITY
Answer: Since deciding to specialize in growing nectarines, everything was—PEACHY KEEN

109. **Jumbles:** GLAZE AGENT DROOPY JARGON
Answer: The display at the Levi Stauss museum showed the dungarees'—"JEAN-EALOGY"

110. **Jumbles:** MANLY STASH CUDDLY PONCHO
Answer: After explaining to his parents that he was going to be a mime, they said—YOU DON'T SAY

111. **Jumbles:** HYENA GRAND DRENCH DISOWN
Answer: Being dealt a royal flush and winning—GO HAND IN HAND

112. **Jumbles:** VIPER BASIC DECADE TURKEY
Answer: Yet again, Keesterman's mailbox gets—"BUS"-TED

113. **Jumbles:** LUNGE WHINE CAUGHT GUITAR
Answer: When the robot experienced abdominal surgery, it was—GUT-WRENCHING

114. **Jumbles:** BLOAT PATIO SLEEPY MARKET
Answer: Drinking coffee after three o'clock caused Susan a—"LATTE" PROBLEMS

115. **Jumbles:** LOTTO PRONE INVOKE PATCHY
Answer: When young Rube Goldberg wanted to catch a mouse, he built a—CON-"TRAP"-TION

116. **Jumbles:** TIPSY DRAWN WARMLY DEBATE
Answer: After Tía Carmen forgot to stuff her baked treats, Baldo called them—EMPA-"NADAS"

117. **Jumbles:** NERDY BRICK DEFIER HAZARD
Answer: One of the drawbacks of a polar bear's diet—BRAIN FREEZE

118. **Jumbles:** VINYL TINGE PEACHY FIZZLE
Answer: The conceited actress had a special dressing room and was showing off her—VANITY

119. **Jumbles:** SALAD SOGGY SOOTHE BURROW
Answer: The sod company's approach to getting new business was—GRASS-ROOTS

120. **Jumbles:** THANK WORRY CATTLE DEFUSE
Answer: Twitter has a character limit so that people's posts are—SHORT AND "TWEET"

121. **Jumbles:** BUTTE SKULK VERIFY LIZARD
Answer: The Thanksgiving cooks' conversation became serious when they—TALKED TURKEY

122. **Jumbles:** BOGUS LEAKY TURNIP DEBATE
Answer: They examined the wall in the new gold mine and discovered it was—"LODE"-BEARING

123. **Jumbles:** GULCH NEEDY THROAT WILLOW
Answer: They wanted it to be the best pig roast ever, so they—WENT WHOLE-HOG

124. **Jumbles:** LOFTY SAVOR DECENT UPHILL
Answer: The pony that was getting over a bad cold was a—LITTLE "HORSE"

125. **Jumbles:** SCOFF IGLOO DEFIED BOBBLE
Answer: The movie set in the pizza parlor showed a—SLICE OF LIFE

126. **Jumbles:** GIANT KNELT ICONIC ABSORB
Answer: Financial institutions need your business and are—BANKING ON IT

127. **Jumbles:** RATIO MORPH VIOLET LEEWAY
Answer: Gustave Eiffel was shorter than most Parisians, but he was able to—TOWER OVER THEM

128. **Jumbles:** BRASH TABOO SCARCE FACADE
Answer: The prices for equipment in the surf shop were rising—ACROSS THE BOARD

129. **Jumbles:** PANTS MOOSE SCREWY FACTOR
Answer: His prediction that he'd become a quarterback in the NFL had—COME TO PASS

130. **Jumbles:** MACAW TOTAL MIRROR BITTER
Answer: The truck driver who became a farmer had a—TRACTOR TRAILER

131. **Jumbles:** CRAMP PRUNE CHOOSE STICKY
Answer: When she found out the headphones were on sale, it was—MUSIC TO HER EARS

132. **Jumbles:** WHINY ENTRY HAIRDO WRITER
Answer: Don Larsen's perfect game in the 1956 World Series was a gem,—"THREW" AND "THREW"

133. **Jumbles:** SUITE SCOUT COMPEL THRIVE
Answer: He'd caught his opponent cheating, and now the golfer had a—SCORE TO SETTLE

134. **Jumbles:** GUILD WIDTH FIERCE GOPHER
Answer: Because he'd put on a few pounds, he had to tell the other hikers to—"WEIGHT" UP

135. **Jumbles:** BLAND FRESH PUBLIC DELETE
Answer: The crowd of people attending the Memorial Day parade was—RESPECTABLE

136. **Jumbles:** OPERA OFFER SIMMER BANNER
Answer: They didn't have a specific agenda while visiting Italy's capital, so they could—ROAM ROME

137. **Jumbles:** BLURB WORLD FREELY SIZZLE
Answer: Before starting the new ad campaign, the underwear model was—WELL-BRIEFED

138. **Jumbles:** WHARF SALSA SPLICE SOOTH
Answer: The client had little choice but to listen to her trainer who did things—AS SHE SAW FIT

139. **Jumbles:** JOIST TAUNT BANISH SUPPLY
Answer: The new tuxedo rental store was designed by its owner and—BUILT TO SUIT

140. **Jumbles:** THEFT COUGH BEFORE HELIUM
Answer: After the fire at the barbershop, all the barber could do was—COMB THROUGH IT

141. **Jumbles:** SHIRT NOISY PURSUE EQUATE
Answer: The hiker who always climbed to the summit on her birthday was getting—UP THERE IN YEARS

142. **Jumbles:** GRIME WHACK CICADA PROMPT
Answer: When Penn & Teller stepped onto the stage, they were ready to—WORK THEIR MAGIC

143. **Jumbles:** PERCH EMCEE BEAVER FLATLY
Answer: The tailor specialized in superhero costumes and was—VERY "CAPE-ABLE"

144. **Jumbles:** POISE DINKY LETTER CANARY
Answer: The best pitcher in baseball would stay with his current team if they could—STRIKE A DEAL

145. **Jumbles:** DIMLY BIKER CANOLA RAISIN
Answer: They saw the warning about the grizzlies which they would need to—BEAR IN MIND

146. **Jumbles:** SHIRK SLASH SHREWD NOODLE
Answer: To cash in his winning Belmont Stakes "trifecta" ticket, he'd need to—HOLD HIS HORSES

147. **Jumbles:** HOUSE CRUSH TENDON WOODEN
Answer: The teacher caught the girl with bubble gum in class and—CHEWED HER OUT

148. **Jumbles:** BRISK UPEND SQUIRM CHOSEN
Answer: The underwater science team won a grant thanks to their great—"SUB-MISSION"

149. **Jumbles:** CIGAR THINK GLOBAL ONLINE
Answer: King Arthur's meeting at the Round Table was turning into an—ALL-"KNIGHTER"

150. **Jumbles:** KARAT FRAME DIVERT STYLUS
Answer: Samuel de Champlain helped make Quebec the perfect location—"FUR" TRADE TALKS

151. **Jumbles:** SNACK GRIPE INSIST STURDY
Answer: The U.S. flag was changed in 1960 because Alaska and Hawaii were—RISING STARS

152. **Jumbles:** CHIMP FRONT THORNY ATRIUM
Answer: With her new pottery wheel installed, she was hoping to be able to—TURN A PROFIT

153. **Jumbles:** COVER MERCY QUARTZ FLASHY
Answer: To file for his mosquito repellent patent in 1946, Samuel Gertler started—FROM SCRATCH

154. **Jumbles:** PECAN UTTER BLOTCH ODDEST
Answer: The hay farm was struggling due to high debt and needed to be—"BALED" OUT

155. **Jumbles:** YACHT SCARF CHOOSY KEYPAD
Answer: The couple didn't trust banks and kept their money at home in their—CASH CACHE

156. **Jumbles:** BRISK GRAPH JURIST METHOD
Answer: He didn't win the wine competition, and his remarks afterward were—SOUR GRAPES

157. **Jumbles:** CURVY OUNCE SHODDY MILDER
Answer: Drive-in movie theaters were popular because people flocked to them—IN DROVES

158. **Jumbles:** FLOWN MOOSE SIPHON BUTLER
Answer: Her dinner party was suffering from a—HOST OF PROBLEMS

159. **Jumbles:** MINUS THEME DABBLE PENCIL
Answer: The climbers who worked together in an attempt to reach the summit—TEAMED UP

160. **Jumbles:** FUNGI SOUPY AGENDA MELODY
Answer: They were trying to follow the recipe in the cookbook but weren't—ON THE SAME PAGE

161. **Jumbles:** CATTLE BOUNTY POLLEN ARCADE EQUATE FIERCE
Answer: When Cleopatra kept saying no, they called her this—QUEEN OF "DENIAL" (the Nile)

162. **Jumbles:** GOSPEL BANDIT SYMBOL USEFUL ACCORD INJECT
Answer: How some skiers have been known to jump—TO "CONTUSIONS"

163. **Jumbles:** FORMAT DECEIT VANITY MISFIT BELLOW ANYWAY
Answer: The hypocrite talks on "principles" but acts on this—"INTEREST"

164. **Jumbles:** TOUCHY BOUNCE INBORN AFFRAY DRUDGE HAIRDO
Answer: How does a monster like his potatoes?—"FRENCH-FRIGHT" (French-fried)

165. **Jumbles:** ENTIRE PLAQUE BANISH MALLET LACKEY GIGOLO
Answer: What the angry hen also said while quarreling with her mate, the rooster—I'LL LAY IT ON THE LINE!

166. **Jumbles:** EGOISM PERSON HANDLE FERVOR DISMAY SICKEN
Answer: What a man who speaks with forked tongue probably is—A SNAKE IN THE GRASS

167. **Jumbles:** DOOMED BRONCO ANGINA EITHER JOYOUS IMMUNE
Answer: What all the sailors got when a ship carrying red paint collided with one carrying brown paint—"MAROONED"

168. **Jumbles:** EMPIRE BECAME AIRWAY UPKEEP GOODLY HOTBED
Answer: What she sang after she changed the baby's diapers—"ROCK A DRY BABY"

169. **Jumbles:** FORCED NEGATE BESIDE CALLOW OBJECT FLAGON
Answer: He got fired from his job for lying—TOO LONG IN BED

170. **Jumbles:** AROUND TRAGIC ASYLUM BOTHER JARGON VOYAGE
Answer: His mother-in-law's shortcoming was this—HER "LONG STAYING"

171. **Jumbles:** INSIST OCTANE GYRATE SLEEPY LOUNGE GERBIL
Answer: The weightlifters were in their 70s and 80s, but they were—STILL GOING STRONG

172. **Jumbles:** SPLASH VISION UTOPIA ENGAGE EFFORT HECTIC
Answer: The massage would be over after some—FINISHING TOUCHES

173. **Jumbles:** ICONIC DENOTE MASCOT SCENIC SHREWD EXPAND
Answer: After running out of hot dogs, the food vendor had to make a—CONCESSION SPEECH

174. **Jumbles:** HIATUS HAIRDO EXPERT AVIARY OUTING NEGATE
Answer: She purchased the billboard from someone who was happy to—SIGN IT OVER TO HER

175. **Jumbles:** ARTERY HEAVEN DISMAY TUMBLE PURSUE GARLIC
Answer: When the crustaceans started playing sports on the ocean floor, they had—LEAGUES UNDER THE SEA

176. **Jumbles:** VIOLET IMPAIR INFUSE DISOWN HOOPLA MISFIT
Answer: With seats in the front row on the 50-yard line, they had a great—FIELD OF VISION

177. **Jumbles:** POCKET OUTWIT SHADOW DEGREE BURLAP MIGHTY
Answer: When the Mars colony opened its first restaurant, customers really liked its—GOOD ATMOSPHERE

178. **Jumbles:** SMOOTH PEPPER RUFFLE WIGGLE ENGINE DROWSY
Answer: The janitors' union wanted to make changes and was asking for—SWEEPING REFORMS

179. **Jumbles:** CHUNKY EITHER POWDER COUSIN ABRUPT SHREWD
Answer: The car repairs were going well until the auto mechanic—WRENCHED HIS BACK

180. **Jumbles:** HAGGLE OUTLET CHUNKY FEMALE KITTEN THIRST
Answer: The medieval tavern was open daily until 12 a.m. and served customers—"KNIGHT" AFTER "KNIGHT"